Where Are the Poor?

Princeton Theological Monograph Series

Recent volumes in the series:

Sammy Alfaro
Divino Compañero: Toward a Hispanic Pentecostal Christology

Chung-Hyun Baik
*The Holy Trinity—God for God and God for Us:
Seven Positions on the Immanent-Economic Trinity Relation
in Contemporary Trinitatian Theology*

Friedrich-Wilhelm Marquardt
Theological Audacities: Selected Essays

Victor I. Ezigbo
*Re-imagining African Christologies: Conversing with the Interpretations
and Appropriations of Jesus in Contemporary African Christianity*

Linda D. Peacore
The Role of Women's Experience in Feminist Theologies of Atonement

Hemchand Gossai
Power and Marginality in the Abraham Narrative—Second Edition

Jens Zimmermann
*Being Human, Becoming Human: Dietrich Bonhoeffer
and Social Thought*

Where Are the Poor?

A Comparison of the Ecclesial Base Communities and Pentecostalism—A Case Study in Cuernavaca, Mexico

Philip D. Wingeier-Rayo

With a Foreword by Justo L. González

PICKWICK *Publications* · Eugene, Oregon

WHERE ARE THE POOR?
A Comparison of the Ecclesial Base Communities and Pentecostalism—
A Case Study in Cuernavaca, Mexico

Princeton Theological Monograph Series 153

Pickwick Publications
An Imprint of Wipf and Stock Publishers
199 W. 8th Ave., Suite 3
Eugene, OR 97401

www.wipfandstock.com

ISBN 13: 978-1-60608-901-9

Cataloging-in-Publication data

Wingeier-Rayo, Philip D.

   Where are the poor? : a comparison of the ecclesial base communities and
pentecostalism—a case study in Cuernavaca, Mexico / Philip D. Wingeier-Rayo ;
foreword by Justo L. González.

   Princeton Theological Monograph Series 153

   xii + 164 p. ; 23 cm. Including bibliographical references and index.

   ISBN 13: 978-1-60608-901-9

   1. Pentecostalism — Latin America. 2. Basic Christian communities.
I. González, Justo L. II. Title. III. Series.

BR1644.5.L29 WS4 2011

Manufactured in the U.S.A.

Contents

Foreword

IN THE LAST FIFTY YEARS THE CENTER OF CHRISTIANITY HAS SHIFTED radically. What used to be mostly a Western religion with small outposts in the rest of the world has become a truly worldwide faith, encompassing churches with deep roots in many different cultures, and therefore not nearly as uniform as it used to be. Something similar has happened in Protestantism, which at the beginning of the twentieth century was centered on the North Atlantic, and now—particularly in its Pentecostal mode—is truly a world-wide phenomenon.

While this is mostly due to the explosive growth taking place in Africa, Asia, and Latin America, it is also due to the decline of most forms of Christianity in the lands traditionally known as Christendom. In most countries in Europe, Roman Catholic churches that a generation ago were thriving centers of worship are now museums visited mostly by tourists interested in their architecture and their art. A similar decline in attendance and church participation is quite visible in the traditional Protestant lands of Europe—in Anglican churches in England, Reformed churches in Scotland, the Netherlands, and Switzerland, and Lutheran churches in Germany and Scandinavia. Similarly, in the United States most denominations traditionally known as "mainline"—Methodists, Presbyterians, Episcopalians, Lutherans—are also experiencing serious decline in membership and in church attendance.

One result of all this is the tendency of many in the traditional lands of Christendom to think that Christianity is waning. A few years ago a friend who was on sabbatical in England, told me about a distinguished professor at Cambridge University who began a lecture by saying, "Now that Christianity is waning throughout the world . . ." This may be true, but only if Cambridge is the world! Similarly, in many church conventions and nationwide gatherings in the United States one hears a note of malaise and pessimism on the future of the church. Our numbers are declining! We must cut our budgets! If we don't do something soon, we will practically disappear!

It is important for people in the traditional lands of Christendom to put this in its proper perspective. This is not the first time the center of Christianity has shifted. In the early church, it soon moved from Jerusalem to Antioch, and then to an East-West axis along the Mediterranean basin. It then shifted again, now to a North-South axis that led from Rome through the Carolingian lands and on to the British Isles. And then, in connection with the colonial expansion of the sixteenth and nineteenth centuries, to a new East-West axis across the Atlantic Ocean. Thus, if the center is now moving—if it in fact has moved—away from us, this is simply a continuation of a long process. And, if we find this hard to understand or to accept, it is because we took for granted that we were the final and definitive step in the process, and now we must learn that it is not so, and figure out what our new role is in the new world-wide church.

This is why studies in world Christianity have become so important in our day. Half a century ago, most seminaries in the United States—and several programs of theological education in Europe—included courses on "missions." In those courses students explored ways to communicate the gospel in other cultures and settings. It was taken for granted that missions were unidirectional, from the Christian West to the rest of the world. Missions were not so much a theological as a practical field of study. We knew what the church was. We knew what proper doctrine was. It was now a matter of learning how to communicate all this to the rest of the world. But now the task is different. Now there are more Protestant Puerto Rican pastors serving in New York City and its environs than all the missionaries sent out to all the world by all the missionary agencies in New York. Now there are Korean, Ugandan, and Brazilian missionaries in California, England, and Ireland. Now the question is no longer, how can we communicate the faith to other nations and cultures, but rather, how are we to understand our own faith and our own church life in the light of what is taking place throughout the world. Unlike the former courses on missions, today's courses on world Christianity are profoundly theological, asking questions such as: What does the church experience of Christians in Korea tells us about the nature and mission of the church? What do new forms of worship in Kenya and in Brazil tell us about the nature of worship? What does the incarnation of Christianity in so many cultures tell us about its incarnation in our own culture?

For all these reasons, studies on Christianity in other parts of the world are of paramount importance for the church in the United States and Europe. It is not just a matter of gaining solace from knowing that there are places where the Christianity is doing well. It is also a matter of gaining a deeper understanding of what may be the future shape of the church, both in the traditional lands of Christendom and in the rest of the world.

It is at this point that the present study becomes important. For English-speaking readers, it is not just a matter of curiosity about two phenomena that have come to the foreground in Latin American Christianity. It is also a matter of looking at such movements and seeking to discern what they tell us about world-wide Christianity, and about our own role within it.

Each of the two movements compared in this study has received wide attention. The *Comunidades eclesiales de base* (CEBs), which emerged in Latin American Catholicism in connection with Liberation theology, have been studied for their methodology, for their hermeneutics, for their relationship—both positive and negative—with church hierarchy, and for their undeniable impact on the renewal that is currently taking place in Latin American Catholicism. Pentecostalism has been studied mostly for its explosive growth, to the point that some are even suggesting that at the present rate Latin America will soon become mostly Protestant. CEBs have been praised by the place of lay leadership within them, for the originality of their thoughts and actions, and for the solidarity they engender among their members. Pentecostalism has been praised as lifting many of the destitute from abject poverty, as giving uprooted urban masses a place of belonging and community, and as raising its followers' sense of self-worth. CEBs have been criticized as ideological arms of left-wing revolutionary movements, as subtle means of getting people to come to the conclusions that their leaders desire, but particularly for undermining the traditional authority of the hierarchy. (Indeed, many analysts claim that the real reason why under the leadership of Cardinal Ratzinger—now Pope Benedict—two stern warnings were issued against Liberation Theology was not so much that it made use of Marxist analysis, as that the CEBs undercut the authority and control of the hierarchy.) Pentecostalism, on the other hand, has been criticized for being other-worldly, for not being concerned with issues of social justice, for being authoritarian, and for being divisive, as it both pulls people away from mainstream society and becomes splintered within its own ranks.

Dr. Wingeier-Rayo's study deals with these matters. But, rather than generalizing about CEBs and about Pentecostalism as they appear throughout Latin America, he focuses on two faith communities in Cuernavaca, a CEB and a Pentecostal church. While taking full cognizance of the dissimilarity between the two, he also shows that there are many points of contact, and that the current stereotypes about both CEBs and Pentecostal churches need to be questioned or at least nuanced. While there are significant differences, these are not what one would expect on the basis of general reports on these two movements. Thus, the reading of this book will produce a more careful and balanced understanding of both CEBs and Pentecostalism.

Some might object that, by focusing on two specific communities in a single city, the author risks presenting the particular as if it were general. But Dr. Wingeier-Rayo is very careful in delimiting and clarifying the purpose of this study, and makes clear that he does not expect all CEBs nor all Pentecostal churches to be like the ones he has studied. However, on the basis of what I have observed in various parts of Latin America, I have no doubt that similar studies in other areas would frequently yield similar results.

I have stated elsewhere that the two great theological subjects for Christian theology in the twenty-first century are the doctrine of the Holy Spirit and eschatology. Common wisdom tends to think of these—particularly the doctrine of the Spirit—as central to the Pentecostal movement. This is certainly the case; but what is not as widely noted is that the same is true, albeit in a different way, of CEBs. While most CEBs are not "charismatic" as that word is understood today, some are, and the very existence of CEBs, no matter whether "charismatic" or not, opens the laity to the possibility that the Spirit may work through them, quite apart from the hierarchy. And eschatology, that is, Christian hope, is at the very center of the life of most CEBs, whose work is grounded on the hope and expectation of a better world. It is the combination of these two elements, pneumatology and ecclesiology, that give both Pentecostalism and the CEBs their specific character. Since each of the two movements views these issues in a different way, there are vast differences between. But, since they focus on these two issues, there are also bridges and points of contact that are seldom noticed.

Dr. Wingeier-Rayo's study, focusing on two specific communities of faith, is important not only for what it says about those two communities, but also as a guidepost pointing to similarities and differences not widely noticed. It should serve both as a model for future studies and as a sign that the relationship between these two phenomena in contemporary Christianity is much more complex than is often imagined. I commend him on a work well done, and trust that others will follow his example in seeking to clarify the true nature of worldwide Christianity in the twenty-first century.

Justo L. González

1

Introduction and Hypothesis

Two contemporary ecclesial movements are capturing the attention of the poor in Latin America: the Ecclesial Base Communities and the Pentecostal churches. The former, a renewal movement within the Roman Catholic tradition, has been criticized for being overly political, and even a front for communism. The latter, an outgrowth of the nineteenth-century North American holiness movement, has been accused of being an opiate of the people that offers an escape from the harsh realities of Latin America. Frequently, both movements work among the same sectors of society, and even in the same *barrios*. Why would some people choose to participate in an Ecclesial Base Community and others, seemingly of the same socio-economic background, choose to join a Pentecostal church? How is it that these seemingly contradictory movements come from the same the Latin American context? Are Base Christian Communities indeed a political organization, or do they have a spiritual foundation? And similarly, are Pentecostal churches a vehicle for escapism or do their members develop social consciousness and empowerment to confront social injustice?

These questions have become urgent to me as I have traveled and worked in Latin America over the last two decades. During the late 1980s in Nicaragua, I had the privilege to work with the *Comunidades Eclesiales de Base* (CEBs) that I will refer to by their Spanish acronym CEBs from here on. These neighborhood-based Bible study and reflection groups were interpreting the gospel in light of the revolutionary context in which they were living.[1] Prior to the 1979 triumph of the Sandinista Revolution, the CEBs understood the oppression and injustice imposed by the Somoza dictatorship to be against the principles

1. Cardenal, *Gospel in Solentiname*, 1:242.

of the gospel. Therefore they engaged in protests, strikes, and in some cases directly supported the Sandinista guerrilla army with food and shelter. Some of the CEB's young men and women joined the Sandinista movement as an outgrowth of their faith.

I lived in Nicaragua while the Sandinista government was in power—a time of great revolutionary fervor. The government was promoting health care, education and land reform with the support of the masses. Young people across the country had participated in vaccination and literacy campaigns, predominantly among the rural poor. The CEBs had enthusiastically supported these reforms as signs of the Kingdom of God and were developing their own social service projects to complement the government programs. In Managua, the CEBs had a network of local Bible study groups working in twenty-three different neighborhoods. Their interpretation of the gospel had moved them to begin alternative health care and nutrition projects among the poor in five Managua *barrios*. They promoted homeopathic medicine and highly nutritious soy food as low-cost alternatives for the poor. Part of their service involved the purchase of basic staple foods in the countryside to be distributed in the poor urban neighborhoods at cost.

The CEBs developed a worldwide solidarity network in Europe, North America and Latin America where they received economic and moral support. Sometimes they received donations of used clothes and distributed them for a minimal fee in the *barrios*. As I participated in these service projects in addition to Bible studies, retreats and seminars, I developed a deeper social consciousness that was transformative for my personal spiritual journey.

After this paramount experience working in Nicaragua for two years, I was assigned (after a two-year stint in the Rio Grande Valley, Texas) to yet another revolutionary context. The other Latin America country to undertake a popular revolution was the island nation of Cuba in 1959. I went to Cuba with all my expectations and baggage from the revolutionary experience of Nicaragua. However, I found a very different context. In 1991 the Cuban revolution was in its 32nd year and the early revolutionary spirit had all but died out. To make matters worse, in August of that same year the Soviet Union experienced a *coup d'état* and Mikael Gorbachev stepped down as president. The Soviet Union dissolved and unilaterally reneged on its favorable trade agreements with Cuba. Without these financial subsidies, Cuba's economy was on the verge of collapse and no major trade partners emerged to fill the void, making the decade of the 1990s extremely difficult for Cubans.

The religious landscape was also quite different in Cuba. The revolution had occurred in 1959 before the second Vatican Council, the Council of Bishops meeting in Medellin, and the emergence of liberation theology. Therefore the churches, both Protestant and Catholic, were not welcome in the revolutionary process. The government viewed the church as a partner with the counterrevolutionary movement, and, as such, an ally with the United States government and Cuban exiles. Yet by the late 1960s the church and the state had both realized that neither were going to disappear any time soon (although initially some on both sides hoped precisely that) and the government established an Office of Religious Affairs to deal with church-state relations.[2] The Methodist Church in Cuba, to which I was assigned, was largely a product of U.S.-based missionary efforts.[3] After experiencing a crisis in the 1960s and 1970s, the Methodist Church was undergoing a charismatic renewal from traditional Protestant to a quasi-Pentecostal worship style. During the decade of the 1990s, the attendance in the Methodist Church grew from 10,000 to 40,000 and has continued to grow since.

My personal reaction to the worship style was, at first, disdain and suspicion. I had come from a progressive United Methodist background that favored the social gospel over spiritual emotionalism. This was compounded by the revolutionary experience in Nicaragua that emphasized liberation theology and social justice. In spite of this early prejudice, Cuban Christians earned my respect for their endurance during very difficult conditions and for their contagious enthusiasm for the gospel. Over the course of time, I even became impressed by the transformative power of the Pentecostal experience that seemed to sustain and empower people to have hope in the midst of dire circumstances.

As a result, I found myself in the midst of two apparently contradictory, yet perhaps valid, interpretations of what it means to be a Christian in two revolutionary contexts. But I learned that one does not necessarily have to be in two different countries to see these contrasting

2. Wingeier-Rayo, "El Avivamiento," 27.

3. Cubans exiled in the Florida keys, Enrique Someillan and Andres Silveira, returned to Cuba in 1883 to start the first Methodist mission in Havana. After the Spanish-American War in 1898, U.S. missionaries were officially sent to strengthen and expand the Cuban mission throughout the island. See *La Disciplina*, v.

faiths. During my field work in Mexico, I found these two movements existing, even flourishing, side-by-side in the same neighborhood—with different objectives, yet both calling themselves Christian. This phenomenon led me to ask: Why would some people choose to attend a CEB while others, sometimes members of the same family, choose to join the other? The CEBs claim to be a church of the poor within the liberation theology movement that has made a "preferential option for the poor." Are they really working among the poor? The Pentecostals claim to be worshipping a God who can deliver them from suffering, but does conversion to Pentecostalism translate into better life conditions? Are there similarities between the movements which make them more similar than different?

This investigation will move beyond easy answers and stereotypes as it explores these questions and examines the central theme of how each movement relates to the poor. I hypothesize that Pentecostal churches are actually working with a more marginalized sector of the Mexican population than the CEBs. I would also like to test the theories of Emilio Willems, David Martin, David Stoll and others, as to the effects of Pentecostalism on Latin America in a specific context within Mexico—namely, that Pentecostalism is contributing toward the pluralization, democratization and modernization of the Mexican society.[4] I would also like to suggest that the CEBs contribute to democratization, however on a much smaller scale due to the smaller size of their movement and the resistance from the Roman Catholic hierarchy.

As I write I am mindful of the on-going debate among scholars about Ecclesial Base Communities, Pentecostalism and the relationship between the two in Latin America. In an attempt to place my research in dialogue with past and current scholars, I will begin with a review of literature in Part I. This first section contains three chapters, the first of which examines the origin and context of Ecclesial Base Communities in Latin America in general, and Mexico specifically. The structural inequalities and military dictatorships in the 1960s and 1970s, in addition to the progressive changes in the Roman Catholic Church, created a climate conducive to Ecclesial Base Communities and liberation theol-

4. These sociologists refer to pluralization, democratization and modernization in the classical sense of these terms. They find that Pentecostalism promote values of self-discipline, individual initiative, and participatory decision-making among the believers. These values are consistent with the principles of modernization.

ogy. The theoretical literature of Leonardo Boff and Juan Luis Segundo is examined to understand the theological and methodological shifts applied within the CEBs. Bishop Mendez Arceo's leadership in Vatican II, the Latin American Council of Bishops, and in his home diocese of Cuernavaca, was instrumental in the establishment and growth of the CEB network. This second chapter then turns to the history and development of the CEBs in Cuernavaca as a background for my ethnographic research in this region.

Chapter 3 examines the birth and growth of Pentecostalism. This review of background literature explores the origin of the movement and alludes to the heated debate between scholars of Pentecostalism on the roles of Charles Fox Parham, William J. Seymour and the Azusa Street Revival. Spreading to Chile and Brazil, the origin and development of Pentecostalism in Latin America in general, and Mexico specifically are traced. Then the chapter turns to analysis of the phenomenal growth of Pentecostalism in Latin America. The work of two leading sociologists, Christian Lalive D'Epinay and Emilio Willems, is reviewed to establish two leading paradigms. Lalive D'Epinay argues that Pentecostal growth in Latin America is an attempt to reconstruct the traditional *hacienda* system of society, following a period of social *anomie*.[5] In contrast, Willems contends that conversion to Pentecostalism is a symbolic protest against the traditional unjust structure and offers an egalitarian vision leading to the modernization, pluralization and democratization of society.

These two leading paradigms have established the parameters of the contemporary debate led by scholars such as David Martin, David Stoll, Cecilia Mariz, Francisco Cartaxo Rolim, and Jean-Pierre Bastian—each building upon and nuancing earlier positions. Chapter 3 concludes by relating these contemporary interpretations to my thesis about the poor, empowerment, and political involvement.

Chapter 4 compares and contrasts the theoretical interpretations of Base Ecclesial Communities and Pentecostalism. This final chapter of Part One places the theoretical literature about both movements in dialogue with each other and explores their similarities and differences. Concerned with the characteristics of those who elect to join each movement, this chapter also studies the eventual effects of participation

---

5. See chapter 2, "Analysis of Pentecostalism," for a discussion of this phenomenon.

upon the constituency. Thus, this background discussion by scholars of Pentecostalism provides a backdrop and suggests some possible themes to examine for the ethnographic research reported in Part Two.

While the first part provides a theoretical overview of the ongoing discussion about Base Ecclesial Communities and Pentecostalism, the second part tests the theories with concrete case studies. Given the diversity of histories and cultures throughout the different regions in Latin America, any theory about the growth of Pentecostalism is not necessarily applicable to all regions, but needs to be tested. For the same reason, one ethnographic study in one community at a given time cannot presume to have universal implications. This study, therefore, utilizes two methodologies, theoretical and ethnographic, as a check and balance against each other. Both tools are employed to explore these basic questions: What types of people are attracted to each movement? What is the impact of their participation on their lives and on the surrounding community?

PART ONE

Review of Background Literature

2

The Background of Pentecostalism

Introduction

HARVEY COX ASKS AT THE BEGINNING OF HIS BOOK *FIRE FROM HEAVEN*: "Why did Presbyterians, Methodists, and Episcopalians seem to be losing members—down 20 to 40 percent in the [last] twenty-five years . . . while certain other churches, mainly Pentecostal ones, had doubled or tripled their memberships in the same period."[1] Cox makes the point that Pentecostalism has been wrongly ignored by mainline Protestantism as a minority form of Christianity, but that time has now passed. One of the reasons Pentecostalism has been disregarded is that it is seen as a merely vertical expression of the Christian faith that seeks a personal relationship with God without ethical responsibility. Relatively recent reports of Pentecostal involvement in politics have raised questions as to whether this stereotype is accurate. Some scholars of Pentecostalism in Latin America have even characterized Pentecostalism as a religion which identifies with the needs of the poor.[2] This is in contrast to the mainline Protestant churches in Latin America who have attracted principally middle-class members.[3] Does Pentecostalism fit into the stereotypes or does it have an ethical component? Are the poor more attracted to Pentecostalism? This chapter will address these questions by reviewing the origins of Pentecostalism in the United States and its arrival and development in Latin America, specifically Mexico. Then it will examine leading theories about the growth of Pentecostalism and its relationship to the poor.

1. Cox, *Fire from Heaven*, xv.
2. Mariz, *Coping with Poverty*, 8.
3. Lugo, "Ética Social Pentecostal," 107. (Also see d'Epinay, *Religión e Ideología*.)

Context in the United States at the Turn of the Century

The emergence of the Pentecostal movement cannot be understood as separate from the social and religious context of the United States at the end of the nineteenth century. The revivalism and camp meetings of the second Great Awakening in the United States were giving way to the social gospel movement. Following the Civil War, a period of reconstruction led to a sense of optimism and idealism that pervaded the social and religious fiber of America.[4] It was also a time of optimism for the eradication of social ills. American Protestants responded to late nineteenth century social problems such as alcoholism, child labor, and urban slums with various programs and movements. The nineteenth century was declared to be the "Christian Century" in which missionaries of the Christian countries would complete the task of evangelizing the "heathens" of the non-Christian world.

However, the religious response to these issues became divided over theological/doctrinal issues. Revivalism had developed into the holiness movement that thrived largely within the Wesleyan tradition and believed that Christian perfection occurred in a second complete and instantaneous act subsequent to conversion. The majority of the new holiness churches, many of which would become Pentecostal after the Azusa Street revival, were organized in the four years following the 1894 General Conference of the Methodist Episcopal Church, South.[5] The Social Gospel tradition, on the other hand, emphasized the gradual work of sanctification in the individual and the revelation of God in the progressive history of humankind, thus working for structural changes in society. Methodist historian Charles Yrigoyen, Jr. interprets the holiness movement as being "incompatible" with the social gospel movement and supposes that it was this incompatibility that explains the separation of many holiness churches from the Methodist Episcopal Church.[6]

Pentecostal theologian and educator Cheryl Bridges Johns offers a different interpretation. In her view, the holiness movement developed out of a perceived abandonment by Methodism of the cause of

---

4. Yrigoyen, "New Challenges—1865 to 1913," 98.

5. Synon, *Holiness-Pentecostal Tradition*, 48.

6. Yrigoyen, "New Challenges—1865 to 1913," 100.

the masses and the quest for personal piety.[7] She also bridges the instantaneous vs. progressive sanctification debate by adding the element of transformation: "Sanctification thus became a process of consciousness raising whereby people answered God's call to a holy life and to co-create with God in the transformation of society."[8] Johns goes on to observe that unlike the social gospel movement, the holiness movement and these new churches began among the poor.

The aftermath of slavery and black spirituality also influenced the social and religious landscape at the turn of the century. As slaves were traded into slavery against their will, they adapted to Christianity without being completely divested of their African religious heritage:

> White Christian slave traders and missionaries stole Africans from their homeland and disrupted their connections to the family of spirits and religious worldview of the African continent. Furthermore, these traders and missionaries forced speakers of different African languages to commingle, which weakened the memory of Africans as succeeding generations distanced themselves from their ancestral homelands and traditions. Yet enslaved Africans and African Americans retained some practices of African indigenous religions.[9]

One of the means by which black experience of oppression and resistance is preserved and communicated to American society is through the music of "spirituals" and worship style. The black experience and music is one of several early influences upon Pentecostalism.

Origins of Pentecostalism

The early Pentecostal movement in the United States was a mixture of the holiness movement, revivalism, millennialism, Methodism and black spirituality. Pentecostalism began when former Methodist and holiness preacher Charles Fox Parham started Bethel Bible College in Topeka, Kansas in October of 1900. After the first term, Parham asked the students to study the Bible for evidence of the baptism of the Holy Spirit, and on January 1, 1901, the students reported that: "the bibli-

7. Johns, *Pentecostal Formation*, 65.

8. Ibid., 66.

9. Hopkins, *Black Theology of Liberation*, 17.

cal evidence was speaking in tongues as the Spirit gave the utterance."[10] After this experience, Parham closed the Kansas school to travel and teach that the "initial evidence" of receiving the baptism of the Holy Spirit was speaking in tongues. Parham's doctrinal foundations were the basis of the modern Pentecostal movement.[11] In 1905 he settled in Houston and opened another Bible school where he would meet the figure who would join him and share in the founding of Pentecostalism.[12]

William J. Seymour was a student of Parham's at his Houston Bible school before heading up the most notable early Pentecostal revival. Seymour, born in Louisiana to ex-slave parents, was introduced to the holiness views in Indianapolis where he attended a Bible training school and was a member of an African Methodist Episcopal Church. From 1900 to 1902 he attended God's Bible School in Cincinnati and joined a Church of God[13] that was known for its openness to people of all races. In 1905 he traveled to Houston to attend Parham's Bible school. Because of segregation laws, Seymour was forced to sit outside the classroom and listen to lectures in the hallway.[14] Certainly the millennial utopian vision of the holiness-Pentecostal tradition was attractive to a society scarred by racial segregation. Walter Hollenweger, a Norwegian scholar on Pentecostalism, notes the impact of Seymour's African-American heritage upon Pentecostalism:

> The roots of Seymour's spirituality lay in his past. He affirmed his black heritage by introducing Negro spirituals and Negro music into his liturgy at a time when this music was considered inferior and unfit for Christian worship. At the time he steadfastly lived out his understanding of Pentecost. For him Pentecost meant more than speaking in tongues. It meant to love in the face of hate, to overcome the hatred of a whole na-

10. Burgess and McGee, *Dictionary of Pentecostal and Charismatic Movements*, 860.

11. There is currently an intense debate among scholars of Pentecostalism as to who was the founder of Pentecostalism. Parham is credited with teaching that speaking in tongues is the "initial evidence" of receiving the baptism of the Holy Spirit, yet some scholars are hesitant to award him the credit for starting the movement since he did hold membership in the KKK and was latter arrested for unethical behavior.

12. Hollenweger, *Pentecostals*, 338.

13. This is The Church of God that has its headquarters in Anderson, Indiana.

14. Synan, *Holiness-Pentecostal Tradition*, 93.

tion by demonstrating that Pentecost is something very different from the success-oriented American way of life.[15]

Therefore he took Parham's teachings of speaking in tongues as "initial evidence" with him to Los Angeles where he was invited to pastor a congregation.

Neely Terry was another student of Parham's school, and when she returned to Los Angeles she recommended that her church, a black holiness mission, invite Seymour as their pastor. After preaching his first sermon on Acts 2:4 and speaking in tongues, Mrs. Julia Hutchins, president of the church, felt that this teaching was contrary to accepted holiness views and padlocked the church door to keep Seymour out. Therefore Seymour began offering services with a group of black domestic servants and custodial employees in the living room of one of the members at 214 Brae Street in Los Angeles.[16] On April 9, 1906, Seymour and seven others fell to the floor in a religious ecstasy, speaking in tongues.[17] As the crowds grew, Seymour and a group of followers rented a former AME church at 314 Azusa Street where he began the Pacific Apostolic Faith Movement. He held the first service on April 14, 1906, and the *Los Angeles Times* reported "a weird babble of tongues" amid "wild scenes" in the service.[18]

In addition to the gifts of the Spirit, the Azusa Street revival was unique in its integration of blacks and whites in the same congregation.[19] This occurred at a time when "Jim Crowism," racial segregation, and white supremacy were prominent in American society, particularly amongst poor whites and poor blacks.[20] The prophetic call for a utopian vision of society in the face of current inequalities was strongly encouraged in early Pentecostalism.

> There can be no doubt that in its early stages the Pentecostal movement was completely interracial. The Azusa Street meeting was conducted on the basis of complete racial equality.

15. Hollenweger, cited in Synan, *Holiness-Pentecostal Tradition*, 167.

16. Cox, *Fire From Heaven*, 45.

17. Synan, *Holiness-Pentecostal Tradition*, 96.

18. Burgess and McGee, *Dictionary of Pentecostal and Charismatic Movements*, 780.

19. Hollenweger, "Charismatic and Pentecostal Movements," 209.

20. Synan, *Holiness-Pentecostal Tradition*, 167.

Pentecostalism pointed out that just as the first Pentecost recorded in Acts 2:1–11 included "men out of every nation under heaven," the modern "Pentecost" at Los Angeles included people of every racial background.[21]

There were reports of blacks, whites, Mexicans, Italians, Chinese, Russians, and Indians participating together in the Azusa Street revival.[22] These radical egalitarian roots and this utopian vision of society are a part of Pentecostalism's legacy.

Pentecostalism has often been confused with fundamentalism, but the terms are not synonymous, nor do they have similar origins.[23] Fundamentalism began in the 1920s as a reaction against the liberal-modern paradigm, whereas Pentecostalism, as we have seen, predates fundamentalism as an outgrowth of the holiness movement. Quite distinctly, William J. Seymour, utilizing elements of the holiness movement, black spirituality and millennialism, launched a Pentecostal movement with a utopian, egalitarian, interracial vision of society.

The events of Azusa Street immediately spread to other places around the world. Norwegian Methodist pastor T. B. Barrett was on tour in the United States in 1906–1907 when he heard of the revival. He began to correspond with Seymour and took the Pentecostal experience back to Oslo before spreading the movement to Sweden, Denmark, Germany, France, and England.

William H. Durham had been baptized by the Holy Spirit at Azusa Street in 1907 before traveling to Chicago to open the North Avenue Mission.[24] There he played a key role in training leaders to extend Pentecostalism to Latin America. After visiting W. H. Durham's mission in Chicago in 1907 and receiving reports from rising Pentecostal movements around the world, Methodist missionary Dr. Willis C. Hoover

21. Ibid., 170.

22. Ibid.

23. Fundamentalism is a movement which reached its height in the 1920s in the United States as a reaction to liberalism and modernism. With its roots in nineteenth century millenarianism, fundamentalism stresses the inerrancy of Scripture as the final and complete authority for faith and practice. It also preaches a conservative lifestyle of abstinence from alcohol, tobacco, drugs and participation in "worldly entertainment." Although fundamentalism began after Pentecostalism, it has sometimes been confused or mixed with Pentecostal doctrines and behavioral expectations. See Burgess and McGee, *Dictionary of Pentecostal and Charismatic Movements*, 324.

24. Synan, *Holiness-Pentecostal Tradition*, 132.

introduced the experience of "baptism of the Holy Spirit" to his church in Valparaiso, Chile in 1909.[25] Durham's North Avenue Mission would later train two Swedish immigrants, Gunnar Vingren and Daniel Berg, who went to Brazil as missionaries in April of 1911 to spearhead the Brazilian Pentecostal movement.[26] This denomination was called the *Asembleias de Deus*—a denomination constituted in Brazil before the Assemblies of God in the United States[27]—which grew to 680,000 members by 1950 and 1.4 million by 1967.[28] The Pentecostal movement, needless to say, has continued to spread rapidly throughout Latin America and the world.

Today it is believed that there are between 400 and 500 million Pentecostals in the world.[29] Of the reported 75 million Protestants in Latin America, 75 percent are Pentecostals, a percentage which has risen from a mere 25 percent in 1950.[30] While the origins and development have varied according to the particular country or denomination, nevertheless the overwhelming growth is a trend that can not be ignored.

Although the traditional mainline Protestant denominations (e.g. Methodists, Lutherans, Episcopalians, and Presbyterians) arrived first in Latin America, their mission style and presence have been quite different. For the most part, historical Protestants have tended to work among the middle-class sectors of Latin American society, while Pentecostalism exists mainly among the working and lower class made up of peasants, laborers, indigenous, students and the unemployed.[31]

25. Pablo Deiros and Carlos Mraida, *Latinoamérica en Llamas*, 59.

26. Daniel Berg and Gunnar Vingren, two Swedish immigrants, joined Durham´s congregation in Chicago before traveling to the city of Belem to share the Pentecostal doctrine in a previously established Baptist congregation. During a prolonged absence, the pastor left Berg in charge. When he returned he found his church practicing a Pentecostal doctrine and promptly expelled Berg and Vingren. Irregardless the church split and the two missionaries launched the Pentecostal movement in Brazil. See Hollenweger, *Pentecostals*, 75.

27. The Assemblies of God was formed in 1914 when small independent Pentecostal churches who believed in the doctrine of "Finished Work" felt the need to start a unified organization which would provide a denominational home. Synan, *The Holiness-Pentecostal Tradition*, 153.

28. Hollenweger, *Pentecostals*, 78.

29. Cleary, "Introduction," in Cleary and Stewart-Gambino, *Power, Politics, and Pentecostals in Latin America*, 1.

30. Deiros and Mraida, *Latinoamérica en Llamas*, 14.

31. d'Epinay, *Religión e Ideología*.

Whereas the mainline Protestant missions started schools and hospitals, Pentecostals avoided these administrative and financial burdens by spreading through the practice of informal, grass-roots evangelism in poor neighborhoods.

Many observers initially felt that this was an invasion of North American sects. While it is true that there have been North American missionary efforts, there have also been many autonomous and spontaneous church plants in Latin America. Many Pentecostal denominations have indigenous leadership and have developed their own financial base.[32] It is common for Pentecostal members to give 10 percent of their income and sometimes even more financial support. Hollenweger cites some examples of the benefits of Pentecostal self-sufficiency:

> The self-help programs of the Kimbanguists in the Congo or the Indian Pentecostals in Mexico may look primitive to an expert of the UNO or Christian Aid, but the advantage is that they have invented the programs themselves. They have financed themselves. They do not depend on foreign skill, personnel or spare parts. They have become aware of their own dignity. There is a process of democratization in their worship services.[33]

While some Pentecostal sects have been highly subsidized by their U.S. counterparts, still others are autonomous or nearly self-sufficient. Now I will offer a typology of denominational structures in Latin America who have received their legacy from mother churches in the United States.

Organizational Structure of Pentecostalism

The organizational structure of Pentecostal churches in Latin America is varied. In a dated, but still helpful typology, Eugene A. Nida organizes Latin American churches in four categories: 1) mission-directed churches, 2) "national-front" churches, 3) "indigenized churches," and 4) fully indigenous churches. The mission-directed churches are not indigenous or under local leadership, but are run by expatriates and their foreign mission agencies. "National-front" churches, on the other hand, have figureheads which are the national leadership, but are really directed from abroad. The "indigenized" churches have now broken away from

32. Cleary, "Introduction," 5.

33. Hollenweger in Kirkpatrick, *Holy Spirit*, 222.

foreign "mother" churches to be managed by national leaders. Lastly, fully indigenous churches have grown exclusively with Latin American leadership and are self-funded.[34] The churches in Latin America have different ecclesiologies according to which category they fall under and the organizational structure of the mother church. All these typologies are present in the origins of Pentecostalism in Mexico.

Development of Pentecostalism in Mexico

Four decades after the mainline Protestant mission boards in the United States had established eighteen denominations in Mexico starting in 1872, Pentecostalism crossed the border through family ties when Romana de Valenzuela traveled to Los Angeles in 1912 and experienced a conversion in a house-church. A short time later in a second saving event, she received the Holy Spirit, spoke in tongues, and was baptized together with her husband. From that moment on Mrs. Valenzuela's burning desire was to return to her native Mexico and share her experience. Finally in 1914, she departed for her home town of Villa Aldama in the northern state of Chihuahua. As soon as her family found out that Romana had come back Protestant, their joy turned into rage. Mrs. Nicolaza de Garcia, Romana's sister-in-law, who would later become the first Pentecostal convert in Mexico, recalled that "the arrival of Romana disrupted the home."[35] Nicolaza's son, Miguel, was the first to try to understand the reasons behind Romana's conversion. After a series of prolonged conversations with his aunt, Miguel became convinced that she was trying to teach the truth. Although Miguel was only a young man, he was well respected in the family and convinced the others that Romana had a right to be heard. This opened the door for an intensive Bible study course that Romana had prepared in Los Angeles.

The small group, composed exclusively of Romana's relatives, started to pray fervently and ask for the baptism of the Holy Spirit. On November 1, 1914, the group spoke in tongues. Mrs. Valenzuela now had twelve converts under her direction, but time was short as her husband impatiently awaited her return to Los Angeles. So she began to look for a pastor to baptize the group. She visited Pastor Ruben Ortega of the Methodist Church in Chihuahua—not to become Methodists—but

---

34. Nida, "Indigenous Churches in Latin America," 97.

35. Gaxiola, *La Serpiente y La Paloma*, 4.

to be baptized by immersion to constitute a Pentecostal church.[36] Rev. Ortega listened to Romana's testimony of baptism of the Holy Spirit and agreed to go to Villa Aldama. When he heard the group speaking in tongues he was convinced that it was the Holy Spirit and began to pray with them until he himself had the same experience.

Then Romana traveled with Rev. Ortega to El Paso, Texas, the closest city with a Pentecostal church, where he was baptized in the name of Jesus by an African-American pastor. Rev. Ortega then returned to Villa Aldama as a "Pentecostal" to baptize the first twelve Pentecostal members in Mexico. He led the new group while continuing his preaching in Chihuahua. He did not stay with the congregation too long, however, as accounts indicate that he began to introduce fanatical and extremist practices before eventually losing his mind and passing away.[37] Subsequently, Miguel, Romana's nephew, became the new leader and named the congregation *La Iglesia Evangélica Espiritual*. This remained the name until 1928 when it adopted its current name, *La Iglesia Apostólica de México*.[38]

Shortly after Romana's missionary work in Chihuahua, another Mexican-American woman, Maria W. Atkinson, formerly Maria de los Angeles Rivero, began traveling across the border from Douglas, Arizona to Obregón, Sonora. Maria raised money from friends and relatives to do missionary work. According to sources from *La Iglesia de Dios: Evangelio Completo in Mexico*, she began these travels in 1912, and had four groups meeting in Alamos, Sonora by 1920.[39] After contending against the accusations of other denominations of being a drug-trafficker, a witch, a hypnotist, an old lady promoting prostitution, being possessed by the devil and trying to pass as an American missionary, she finally established a separate denominational structure. Carlos Jimenez was named the first pastor of the group and Rev. Santiago H.

36 Apostolic Pentecostal denominations are know for the doctrine of Oneness, which means that they baptize in the name of Jesus Christ as opposed to the Trinitarian doctrine which baptizes in the name of the Father, Son and Holy Ghost. Jones, "Apostolic Church of Pentecost," in Burgess and McGee, *Dictionary of Pentecostal and Charismatic Movements*, 16.

37. Gaxiola, *La Serpiente y La Paloma*, 5.

38. Ibid., 6.

39. Bonilla, "Breve Historia de Congreso y Asambleas 1932–1972," 6.

Ingram became the superintendent of the work in Mexico. The strategy and doctrine of the movement was:

> to establish work where historical churches have already been established and to proclaim the eternal principles of Pentecost: baptism of the Holy Spirit, with the initial evidence of speaking in other tongues as the Spirit leads (glossolalia), divine healing, holiness, separating oneself for God from the world and its pleasures, and the spiritual gifts manifested in the Church.[40]

The movement established missions throughout the state of Sonora in the towns of Esperanza, Etchojoa, Chucarit, Empale, San Blas and Sinaloa. Under the supervision of Rev. James H. Ingram, in 1932 the first *Iglesia de Dios* was officially organized in Obregon, Sonora—the site of Maria Atkinson's original travels.[41] About that time in central Mexico, a missionary of the Assemblies of God, Anna Sanders, started several congregations with Rev. David G. Ruesga. However, Rev. Ruesga was courted by the *Iglesia de Dios: Evangelio Completo* and eventually switched denominations in an official union on January 25, 1940.[42] In 1941, the denomination *Iglesia de Dios: Evangelio Completo* celebrated its first convention in Mexico.[43]

Although the growth of Pentecostalism was predominantly an urban phenomenon in northern Mexico until the decade of the 1940s, today the movement has spread throughout Mexico and into the rural areas.[44] Due to the industrialization of the Mexican economy after World War II, rural populations began to migrate from the countryside to the cities. Although mainline Protestant denominations were stronger in the early part of the century, statistical reports reveal that membership in Pentecostal churches tripled during each decade from 1940 to 1970 and passed traditional denominations in membership sometime during the 1950s.[45] The growth of Pentecostalism accelerated even more during the 1970s, especially among the migrant and marginalized sec-

40. Ibid., 5.
41. Ibid., 4.
42. Lopez, "Historia de la Iglesia de Dios," 13.
43. Bonilla, "Breve Historia de Congreso y Asambleas 1932–1972," 10.
44. Bastian, *Protestantismo y Sociedad en México*, 223.
45. Ibid., 221.

tors of Mexican society. Today 80 percent of Protestants in Mexico are Pentecostal.[46]

Analysis of Pentecostalism

Two sociologists in the 1960s proposed diverging, yet paradigmatic theories about the origin and growth of Pentecostalism in Latin America. Invited by the World Council of Churches to study the phenomenon, Swiss sociologist Christian Lalive d'Epinay, concluded in his appropriately titled book, *Haven of the Masses: A Study of the Pentecostal Movement in Chile*, that Pentecostalism attempts to recreate the traditional system in times of catastrophic change and uncertainty. D'Epinay based his research on the theories of French sociologist Emile Durkheim who had a stable view of culture. Rescuing an old term coined by Emile Durkheim, Lalive d'Epinay refers to this period of rupture with the traditional cultural system as *anomie*. He defines *anomie* as:

> the result of a gap in the regimentation of the individual in society. . . . The structure of that society, in the security of which the individual used to find support, is in a state of 'rupture', which in turn involves the loss of the consensus that regulates the normative orientation and existential definition which give meaning to the life of the individual or group.[47]

Lalive d'Epinay interprets the decline of the *hacienda* plantation system[48] and the economic crisis of the 1930s in Chile to fit Durkheim's definition of *anomie*. This crisis in traditional society, according to Lalive d'Epinay, coincides with Pentecostal expansion. Therefore, Chile's traditional rural society was reconstructed in Pentecostalism. According to Lalive d'Epinay, the paternalistic and authoritarian structure of the *hacienda* system of rural Chile was recreated in Pentecostalism with the pastor assuming the role of *el patrón*.[49] In the case of migration

---

46. Ibid., 224.

47. d'Epinay, *Haven of the Masses*, 32–33.

48. The *hacienda* system was implemented in Latin America under Spanish colonial rule. One wealthy landowner, *el patrón* (see n. 49), owned a very large plantation and exploited the labor of the peasants who lived on his land and were dependent on him for their livelihood.

49. *El Patrón* is a Spanish word which is loosely translated as "boss" in English, but has much more paternalistic connotations in Spanish and could be translated as "master."

from the countryside to the city, Pentecostalism was the mechanism that helped the migrants retain meaning as they adapted to the *anomie* of urban life. Therefore Pentecostalism, according to Lalive d'Epinay, reproduced the most traditional and conservative features of hierarchy and subordination in society.

Whereas Lalive d'Epinay represents a conservative interpretation of the impact of Pentecostalism upon society, Emilio Willems, who did his research among Pentecostals in Chile and Brazil, concluded that this movement might actually be an opportunity for positive social and political change. Willems bases his theoretical framework on Max Weber's hypothesis of conflict and change that links Protestantism to capitalism.[50] Willems concludes that Pentecostalism makes a contribution toward the modernization and pluralization of Latin American society. Assuming that Pentecostals are part of the Protestant tradition, an assumption that would later be questioned by Swiss sociologist, Jean-Pierre Bastian, Willems notes the democratic values taught by Protestant missionaries in Latin America:

> In light of contrasting Latin American structural principles, the following may be pointed out: the assumption of ethical equality of the members of a community regardless of wealth, educational background, or occupation; the assumption that the individual members of a community are morally and intellectually capable of solving their problems in a responsible fashion; the assumption that leadership does not imply restriction of freedom of expression and judgment. A leader's initiative should be inspired by group opinion; he should help people of course, but above all he should teach people to help themselves.[51]

These are Protestant values, Willems argues, that have advanced modernization and democratization in Latin America.

Noting its fundamental egalitarianism, Willems goes on to propose that not only does Pentecostalism advance democracy, it also challenges the injustice and inequality in the current social order:

> The organizational pattern of the Pentecostal sects seems to express a protest against the Catholic Church and its ally, the

50. Willems, *Followers of the New Faith*, 15, Max Weber argues in his classic book, *Protestant Ethic and the Spirit of Capitalism*, that Protestants who have consecrated their trades to God have advanced modern industrial capitalism.

51. Ibid., 11.

ruling class. It does so by pointedly stressing egalitarianism within the sect and by opposing the Catholic principle of an ecclesiastical hierarchy and a highly specialized priesthood with the principles of the primacy of the laity, the priesthood of all believers and a self-made charismatic leadership sanctioned by the Holy Spirit. Pentecostalism thus turns out to be a symbolic subversion of the traditional social order.[52]

Willems observes that Pentecostalism is a movement in which the layperson is in control of church affairs. Contrary to Lalive d'Epinay's conclusion that Pentecostalism maintains the status quo, Willems argues that conversion is rebellion against traditional social structures and that this participatory system can promote democratization in Latin American society.[53]

These early sociological analyses of Pentecostalism by Lalive d'Epinay and Willems present two different paradigms that have shaped the more recent debates about Pentecostalism. Michael Dodson offers an accurate summary of each position:

> The two writers agreed that Pentecostalism is a religion of the poor, that it offers both psychological security and the minimal material security necessary to cope with a hostile environment, that it affords emotional release more than it challenges the intellect. . . . But whereas Willems saw signs to suggest that Pentecostalism might help promote modernization and democratization, Lalive d'Epinay argued forcefully that the evidence pointed to the opposite conclusion.[54]

These two initial studies have become paradigmatic in subsequent scholarly efforts to understand the phenomenon of Pentecostalism. Later studies have generally appropriated and strengthened one of these two different interpretations.

In line with Willems' hypothesis, British sociologist David Martin agrees that Pentecostalism in Latin America contributes toward the economic and social advancement of society.[55] In his books *Tongues of Fire: The Explosion of Protestantism in Latin America* and *Pentecostalism: the*

52. Ibid., 249.

53. Dodson, "Pentecostals, Politics, and Public Space in Latin America," in Cleary and Stewart-Gambino, *Power, Politics, and Pentecostals in Latin America*, p. 27.

54. Ibid., 26.

55. Martin, *Tongues of Fire*, 228 and *Pentecostalism*.

World Their Parish, the author makes a socio-historical analysis of the implications of Pentecostalism's rapid growth for social change. He contrasts the monolithic culture of control of the predominantly Roman Catholic countries in southern Europe which colonized Latin America with the pluralism of Arminian Protestantism brought to North America by the Northern Europeans.[56] The economic and imperialistic power of the United States has continued to export religion south to Latin America while the monopolistic control of the Roman Catholic Church in Latin America has begun to crack, opening these societies for increasing change. Martin's thesis is that indeed the growth of evangelical Christianity will contribute to the pluralization and social differentiation of Latin America, but cautions as to whether Pentecostals will really be more democratic than Catholics.[57]

David Stoll published another insightful interpretation of Pentecostalism with the suggestive title, *Is Latin America turning Protestant?* Stoll examines the rapid growth of Protestantism in Latin America, but does not offer one easy explanation for its increase. He rejects theories that explain the multiplication of evangelical churches as simply the result of North American funding.[58] More likely, he argues, evangelicalism is a reaction to Roman Catholic clericalism and centralized authority that represses religious pluralism.[59] The author also acknowledges that the majority of the converts are poor, and that evangelicalism offers solace to the victims of war and economic crisis. As a sociologist, Stoll rejects the idea that religion is always a conservative force in society which maintains the status quo. Instead he advocates a dynamic view of religion as a form of social protest.[60] For Stoll the growth of the Protestant movement is a form of protest in Latin American society, which is contributing toward its modernization, democratization and pluralization.

With regard to liberation theology, Stoll criticizes the leaders of liberation theology as being well-educated professionals who are carry-

56. Ibid., 23.

57. Ibid., 294.

58. Stoll, *Is Latin America Turning Protestant?*, xv.

59. Ibid., 25.

60. Ibid., iv.

ing out a political agenda, often at the expense of the poor.[61] Rather, he argues that the true revolution in Latin America may be more private than public: ". . . whereas Marxism tends to spread from the place of work, Pentecostalism tends to spread from the family and home."[62] In spite of this apparent dichotomy, Stoll does recognize the complexity of Pentecostalism and acknowledges that there are many competing interests and factions.

Jean-Pierre Bastian, in contrast, follows Lalive d'Epinay's early analysis of the growth of Pentecostalism. Bastian agrees that Pentecostalism emerges following an *anomie* that provokes a reorganization of society around familiar power structures:

> As a matter of fact, one can observe that its relationship with Protestantism is not fruitful, because these religious movements [Pentecostalism] do not contribute new religious and democratic values to the Latin American political culture. On the contrary, they seem to be carriers of a "patchwork" religiosity and of a political and social behavior whose model proceeds from authoritarian leadership styles and mechanisms of corporate domination.[63]

Bastian goes on to question Pentecostalism's relationship to classical Protestantism: "For this reason, it is appropriate to ask if there is motive to employ the term Protestantism when one refers to these movements [Pentecostalism]. . . ."[64] Bastian outlines the different values taught by Protestants and Pentecostals:

> While the first [Protestantism] was a religion of written, civic and rational education, the later [Pentecostalism] is an oral, semi-illiterate and fervent religion. While the former was a carrier of practical, liberal democratic values, the latter transmits *caudillistic*[65] models of religious and social control.[66]

---

61. Ibid., 312.

62. Ibid., 317.

63. Bastian, *Protestantismo y Sociedad en México*, 278; my translation.

64. Ibid., 291.

65. *Caudillistic* is a Spanish word that has its roots in the pre-Hispanic word *caudillo*, which means "chief." In this context the author uses it to refer to the hierarchical leadership style in pre-Hispanic Mexico.

66. Bastian, *Protestantismo y Sociedad en México*, 300; my translation.

In a more recent article, "The New Religious Map of Latin America: Causes and Effects," Bastian takes a more open posture and writes that it is too premature to assume that Pentecostalism will have an effect on modernization or economic conduct. Here he concludes that we need to carry out serious studies that would allow us to develop a hypothesis about the contribution of Pentecostalism to modernity.[67]

Yet another sociologist, Canadian Kurt Bowen, researched evangelicalism specifically in Mexico and uses a variety of theories and explanations for evangelical growth.[68] Each individual theory is inadequate in itself for explaining such a complex and diverse phenomena. He describes a combination of contributing theories:

> Disorganization, deprivation, and protest have all played a part in Evangelicalism's appeal, but they cannot explain why the discontented, or at least some of them, were drawn to a religious and, specifically, an Evangelical solution to their problems. Part of the answer lies in the recentness of urbanization for so many Mexicans and the prevalence of rural, traditional ways of thinking, where doubts about the presence and power of the supernatural were little developed. Evangelicalism's appeal has also lain in the failure of the Catholic Church to respond to the discontents of its constituency.[69]

Bowen concludes his in-depth study by questioning whether it is truly growing as fast as some proponents indicate. As his title *Evangelism and Apostasy* suggests, Bowen argues that the real growth rate is higher than it appears because the evangelical churches have almost as many dropouts as they do new converts.[70]

While European and North American social scientists offer helpful observations from abroad, Latin American scholars are also well situated as insiders to assess the impact of Pentecostalism upon their own societies. For example, Brazilian sociologist Rubem Cesar Fernandes disagrees with the Lalive d'Epinay paradigm of Pentecostalism as merely a response to the *anomie* of society. He argues that Latin America is

67. Bastian, "New Religious Map of Latin America," 11.

68. Studying several churches across Mexico, Bowen refers to evangelicalism in general, but actually studies a significant number of Pentecostal churches in particular (see 10).

69. Bowen, *Evangelism and Apostasy*, 220.

70. Ibid., 72.

no longer in a period of transition from a traditional agrarian society to capitalism, therefore there are no ruptures or permanent crises contributing to the growth of Pentecostalism.[71]

Chilean theologian, Juan Sepulveda, concurs that Lalive d'Epinay's proposal of *anomie* as a cause is too simplistic. If this were the case, he states, ". . . Pentecostalism would be transitory by essence, and would tend to disappear, or at least stabilize, once the transition was concluded."[72] Clearly this is not the case, as Pentecostalism continues to grow. Brazilian sociologist, Francisco Cartaxo Rolim, agrees that growth is due to much more than just urbanization and migration; one must examine the internal, as well as the external factors. He argues that the majority of the researchers have concerned themselves more with what Pentecostalism *does* in society than what it is.[73] Rolim believes that there is a connection between the growth of Pentecostalism and the restriction of political freedom. Inversely, the growth of Pentecostalism slows when dissatisfaction with the capitalist society is freely expressed. A key element to Rolim's sociological analysis is Pentecostalism's emphasis on non-verbal expressions and symbolic rebellion. He argues in the tradition of Willems, that there is a spirit of protest in Pentecostalism and that speaking in tongues, specifically, is a symbolic protest expressing political discontent.[74] Moreover, Pentecostalism in its complete form, Rolim concludes, is an indirect symbolic challenge to the capitalist system of oppression and unequal distribution of wealth.

Not only does Pentecostalism offer a protest against the current system, it also offers an alternative vision. The eschatological vision of the Reign of God is juxtaposed to the corrupt current order. In Pentecostalism the marginalized sectors of society have the opportunity to visualize an egalitarian society and the oppressed have access to positions of authority and status. Their egalitarian principles and the doctrine of the Holy Spirit allow for any person to be used as an instrument of God: "They were nobody, now they receive special super-

---

71. Fernandes, cited in Droogers, "Visiones Paradójicas," in Barbara Boudewijnse, et al, *Algo Mas Que Opio*, 26.

72. Sepúlveda, "El Crecimiento del Movimiento Pentecostal"; Alvarez, *Pentecostalismo y Liberación*, 84.

73. Ibid., 86.

74. Rolim, *Religiao e Clases Populares*, 172.

natural strength and belong to the chosen."[75] Moreover, the absence of a hierarchy within the Pentecostal church structure, and the potential of all members for charismatic leadership represent a symbolic revolution against the traditional social order. The importance of "prophets" in the Pentecostal congregation allows anyone, regardless of social or educational background, to be a leader in the church:[76]

> The social implications of prophesizing are rather obvious. Vested in religious symbolism, it constitutes a mode of social control which may be exercised by any member of a congregation over anybody else, including the pastor. It minimizes the social distance between the common members and the pastor, between laity and clergy. It is an institutionalized way of keeping authority within the group in a state of continuous flux.[77]

Not only does Pentecostalism present a symbolic protest to the current social order, it also offers an alternative egalitarian model.

In spite of this potential as a force of protest, in the Marxist tradition the Latin American left criticizes Pentecostalism as being an "opiate of the masses."[78] In other words religion, or Pentecostalism in this case, postpones concrete action in response to the injustices of this world to another spiritual world. The hope for an afterlife or paradise in heaven fosters a false expectation that enduring the suffering of this world will earn a reward of eternal life after death.

While Pentecostals do cite the John 18 passage traditionally attributed to Jesus, "my Kingdom is not of this world," John Burdick believes that their faith is integrated into this world. Pentecostalism is a phenomenon that occurs within a specific economic, political and social context. Burdick explains Pentecostals' relationship to the world based on his ethnographic research in Brazil:

75. Hoekstra, "Pentecostalismo Rural en Pernambuco (Brazil)," in Barbara Boudewijnse, et al., *Algo Mas Que Opio*, 50. Also see Willems, *Followers of the New Faith*, 139–44.

76. In Pentecostal congregations it is not uncommon for members to have visions or to portray a message from the divine, thus earning the title of prophet. This is considered to be a spiritual gift of the Holy Spirit.

77. Willems, *Followers of the New Faith*, 139.

78. "Opiate of the Masses" is a phrase made popular by Karl Marx in his critique of religion as inhibiting the proletariat class from organizing against the bourgeoisie.

> Yet the contention that Pentecostals are indifferent to the mate-
> rial world is simply off the mark. . . . Rather than such world-
> renouncing mysticism, most [believers] seek worldly relations
> as marriage, family, work, neighborhood, and the maintenance
> of physical health.[79]

While the theological tendency toward eschatology in Pentecostalism may give the appearance of being "other worldly," the practical applica-tion in the lives of Pentecostals has led to empowerment and change in this life.

As Pentecostals are living and applying their faith in this world, this symbolic or potential protest against the current social order can become manifest political consequences. Replacing the stereotypical apolitical posture of some Pentecostal denominations, more and more Pentecostals are becoming involved in politics: "Today we begin to see cases where the churches depart from an apolitical stance and begin to actively participate in political parties and electoral processes. The question is always on which side and with what ethical principles?"[80] As Evangelical Protestants have become more involved in politics, they have sometimes supported right-wing authoritarian candidates.[81] The most infamous case in Latin America was former military dictator Rios Montt who became president of Guatemala in 1982.[82] Montt, an evangelical Christian, was notorious for ordering the "scorched earth" tactic of persecution against communities who were predominantly indigenous in order to destroy the support base of the guerrilla army. While this is an extreme case, it does show how the evangelical message can take different temporal forms.

Analysts have studied the relationship between the growth of evangelicalism and U.S. foreign policy, particularly U.S. intervention in Central America during the 1980s. The "conspiracy theory"[83] states that the United States government, working through the CIA, has supported evangelical sects to counter the effects of liberation theology and cre-

79. Burdick, *Looking for God in Brazil*, 207.

80. Carmelo, "Panorama Histórico de los Pentecostales Latinoamericanos y Caribeños," in Gutiérrez, *En la Fuerza del Espíritu*, 54.

81. Bastian, *Protestantismo y Sociedad en México*, 296.

82. Ibid., 267.

83. For more on the "conspiracy theory" see Escobar, "Conflict of Interpretations of Popular Protestantism," in Cook, *New Face of the Church in Latin America*, 117.

ate a more amenable pro-U.S. populace.[84] This theory originated during the Reagan Administration's low-intensity conflict policy against the revolutionary movements of the 1980s.[85] The Committee of Santa Fe, which examined U.S. foreign policy objectives in Central America, proposed to the Reagan Administration: "U.S. foreign policy must begin to counter (not react against) liberation theology as it is utilized in Latin America by the 'liberation theology' clergy."[86] Sara Diamond, in her book *Spiritual Warfare: the Politics of the Christian Right*, observes that: "The choice word 'counter' was a signal that a preferred right-wing foreign policy strategy would enlist religious groups in the struggle against popular religious movements critical of U.S. militarism."[87]

Diamond goes on to argue that right-wing evangelical sects were deliberately encouraged by the Reagan Administration as an integral part of low intensity conflict policy against revolutionary movements in Central America:

> "Humanitarian aid" and "psychological operations" are two areas of "total war" where the Christian Right serves U.S. foreign policy objectives best. Acting either as "private" benefactors or as agents of the U.S. government, Christian Right "humanitarian" suppliers and promoters of anti-communist ideology use religion to mask the aggressive, cynical nature of "humanitarian" projects. Cloaked as missionary evangelism, the "spiritual warfare" component of counterinsurgency escapes serious attention by more massive, direct forms of U.S. militarism.[88]

Sara Diamond, Samuel Escobar, and proponents of liberation theology concur that evangelical sects have been utilized (either knowingly or unknowingly) in the larger political matrix of the Cold War in Latin America.

The "conspiracy theory" is helpful in explaining the growth of evangelicalism particularly in the context of the cold war. However, significant world events in the late 1980s and early 1990s have produced

84. Ibid. Also see Stoll, *Is Latin America turning Protestant?*, 139, and Berryman, *Stubborn Hope*, 76.

85. For more on Low Intensity Conflict, see Diamond, *Spiritual Warfare*, 161.

86. The Committee of Santa Fe, "A New Inter-American Policy for the Eighties," 20.

87. Diamond, *Spiritual Warfare*, 147.

88. Ibid., 162. Also see Stoll, *Is Latin America Turning Protestant?*, xiv.

a very different context today. On November 9, 1989, the Berlin Wall came down, uniting East and West Germany; on February 25, 1990 the *Sandinistas* lost national elections in Nicaragua to a coalition of pro-U.S. parties; after initiating *perestroika* in the late 1980s, Gorbachev's administration suffered a *coup d'état* in August of 1991 and the former Soviet Union disintegrated into independent sovereign states. These significant events reshaped power relations in the world, and left the United States as the uncontested hegemonic power in the Western Hemisphere. Although the conspiracy theory may have been an accurate critique of the implicit and explicit role of evangelical sects in U.S. foreign policy, it is not sufficient to explain the continued growth of these movements since the end of the cold war. More than one analyst believes that this is not the case[89] and argues that the remarkable growth and autonomy of Pentecostalism indicates that it is a phenomenon that cannot be explained by only one theory.

In contrast to the religious right's involvement in international politics in Central America, there are also several less well-known cases of Pentecostal ethics encouraging involvement in more progressive local causes.[90] According to Francisco Cartaxo Rolim, in Brazil it was originally the Catholics who organized workers' unions, while the Pentecostal missionaries taught the lower classes to obey the authorities. Yet after the Catholics ended a campaign persecuting Pentecostals, the two groups realized that they had more in common than differences and began to band together in solidarity. Unity allowed them to be a political bloc to act and vote collectively. Therefore, they participated in the workers' unions, the *Ligas Campesinas* for land reform and voted for candidates who offered them greater recognition. According to Cartaxo Rolim, being victims of the Catholic persecution made Pentecostals sensitive to other victims of social injustice, and as a result they joined with rural workers in a common social struggle.[91]

Cecilia Mariz, a sociologist of religion who did her field work in Brazil, agrees that Pentecostals are getting more involved in politics. She

89. Cleary, "Introduction," 5. Also see Stoll, "Is there a Protestant Reformation in Latin America?" 46.

90. Hoekstra, "Pentecostalismo Rural en Pernambuco (Brazil)," in Boudewignse et al., *Algo Mas Que Opio*, 54.

91. Rolim, *O Que e Pentecostalismo*, 75. Also see Shaull and Cesar, *Pentecostalism and the Future*, 226.

argues that Pentecostals struggle for official recognition and power, and therefore participate in politics:

> Although their religion does not encourage them to join so-cial movements, it does not prevent them from joining them. The expansion of these movements and their relative success in obtaining material benefits for the poor have attracted some Pentecostals. In the future, Pentecostals may become more in-volved in such movements. This is highly probable if the trend toward obtaining official recognition and power continues. . . .[92]

Unexpected agreement comes from the late Jesuit liberation theo-logian Ignacio Martin-Baro,[93] who observes: "The political impact of Pentecostalism is complex. On the one hand, the believer, convinced that one has received the Spirit, recuperates a sense of dignity and learns to value one's own manifestations. . . . In this sense, Pentecostalism has been able to support the human and social vindication of the marginalized."[94]

One social area where Pentecostalism has already made a clear im-pact is in gender roles. Although some Pentecostal churches may have a conservative view of gender roles,[95] the latent effect in some cases has been empowerment for women. Elizabeth Brusco, in her book, *The Reformation of Machismo: Evangelical Conversion and Gender in Colombia*, argues that evangelical Protestantism has improved the conditions of the home by facilitating greater domestic involvement of men. As a feminist anthropologist, Brusco's study examines the effect of evangelicalism on the role of women in society. Rather than look-ing at its ideology, she looks at the effect of evangelicalism on women and gender roles: "Unlike Western feminism, it is not attempting to gain access for women to the male world; rather, it elevates domesticity, for both men and women, from the devalued position it occupies as the re-

92. Mariz, *Coping with Poverty*, 113.

93. Father Ignacio Martin-Baro was one of six Jesuit priests assassinated at the Central American University in San Salvador in November of 1989.

94. Martin-Baro, "Del Opio a la Fe Religiosa," in Montero, *Psicología Política Latinoamericana*, 245.

95. There is a broad diversity of teachings with regard to gender roles in Pentecostal denominations. Some denominations accept women pastors, while other denomina-tions maintain the position of Paul with regard to public ministry. Therefore, it is im-possible to generalize about the results of membership to Pentecostalism for women, although the latent effect upon gender roles is a clear trend.

sult of the process of proletarianization."[96] The end effect is to enhance female status with a set of behavioral standards and a community which encourage husbands to assume domestic responsibilities. The result was that the machistic role of the man, who previously spent his income outside the household on alcohol, cigarettes, gambling or other women, was transformed to a responsibility to invest these resources inside the home for the needs of his family.[97] The rhetoric of Pentecostalism may teach traditional gender roles in the home; strategically, however, the result has been to elevate domesticity and empower women.

Pentecostalism has also had an empowering effect upon other marginalized sectors of Latin American society. Even the earliest assessments of Lalive d'Epinay and Willems agreed that it is a religion of the poor.[98] Subsequent scholars have stated that Pentecostalism attracts ". . . mostly the poor, the sick, the unemployed, alcoholics, blacks, and women, who, in general, tend to face more material and emotional hardships."[99] The late liberation theologian Richard Shaull argues that not only is this the case, but that it is intentional:

> Pentecostals address themselves primarily to those who are poor and marginal where they are—overwhelmed by the struggle for survival, in the face of the disintegration of personal and social life. They invite them to open themselves to the realm of the Spirit, entrust their lives to God, and receive power that enables them to respond with new life and energy to all that threatens to destroy them.[100]

Pentecostals are in a good position to offer this support because of their ability to relate to the everyday experiences of the poor. This analysis is similar to Cecilia Mariz's understanding of Pentecostalism as a strategy to cope with poverty.

It is impossible to generalize about the variety of Pentecostal denominations and theologies in so many different contexts across

96. Brusco, *Reformation of Machismo*, 3. Also see Burdick, *Looking for God in Brazil*, 110.

97. Ibid., 5.

98. Dodson, "Pentecostals, Politics, and Public Space in Latin America," in Cleary and Stewart-Gambino, *Power, Politics, and Pentecostals in Latin America*, 26.

99. Mariz and Machado, "Pentecostalism and Women in Brazil," in Cleary and Stewart-Gambino, *Power, Politics, and Pentecostals in Latin America*, 41.

100. Shaull and Cesar, *Pentecostalism and the Future*, 194.

Latin America. There are Pentecostal denominations which may not have undertaken such an intentional outreach to the poor. In addition, there are contradictions and paradoxes within Pentecostalism.[101] The relationship to the world is one of these contradictions. On the one hand, Pentecostals are taught to avoid worldly sins or temptations. On the other, they are very well adapted to function in this world.[102] Likewise, there are egalitarian tendencies, yet the church has hierarchical structures of domination.[103] While there is freedom for emotional expression, there is also a controlling or restrictive discipline. The variety of interpretations may also be due to the observation of distinct Pentecostal denominations in a plurality of geographical locations and socio-economic populations. Given these variables, it is impossible to make definitive statements about the experience of Pentecostals, yet the theories examined in this chapter offer some plausible explanations for the growth of Pentecostalism in Latin America.

Summary

The early studies by European sociologists Christian Lalive d'Epinay and Emilio Willems established two leading paradigms interpreting the phenomenal Pentecostal growth in Latin America. Lalive d'Epinay argued that Pentecostalism was an attempt to reorganize the traditional social order following *anomie*. This approach, supported by Jean-Pierre Bastian, saw Pentecostalism as counterproductive to the modernization of Latin American societies. Emilio Willems, on the other hand, offered a more optimistic assessment, arguing that Pentecostalism, with its egalitarian principles, was a symbolic protest of the current social order.

David Martin and David Stoll supported the hypothesis that Pentecostalism contributes towards pluralization and social change. Kurt Bowen suggested that a variety of theories must be used to explain the growth of Pentecostalism—if indeed it is growing as fast as some advocates indicate. Latin American analysts, such as Francisco Cartaxo Rolim have advanced the theory that Pentecostalism is a symbolic expression of political discontent which grows proportionately to the

101. Doogers, "Visiones Paradójicas," in Boudewijnse et al., *Algo Mas Que Opio*, 39.

102. Ibid., 32.

103. Howe, in Boudewijnse et al., *Algo Más que Opio*, 32.

restriction of political freedom in society. While participation in public issues has resulted in diverging political positions, clearly Pentecostals are becoming more and more involved in politics. Contrary to what some conservative Pentecostal doctrines might suggest, the empowerment of women and the poor who participate in Pentecostalism has been significant. Nevertheless Pentecostalism is too complex a phenomenon to judge with simple generalizations.

3

The Background of the Ecclesial Base Communities

Introduction

LIKE PENTECOSTALISM, ECCLESIAL BASE COMMUNITIES, OR *COMUNI-dades Eclesiales de Base* (CEBs) in Spanish, also emerged in a specific historical period. Unlike Pentecostalism, however, they emerged specifically in Latin America. The economic growth following World War II had polarized Latin American societies creating a small extremely wealthy oligarchy and a large majority of the poor. The 1960s and 1970s were a time of military dictatorships, popular uprisings and revolutionary movements. The church was also in transition following the Second Vatican Council of 1962–1965 creating new opportunities for lay participation. In the midst of this exciting time of change, struggle and hope the CEBs were born. The meetings of Latin American bishops in 1968 in Medellin and 1979 in Puebla affirmed the CEBs. This chapter will explore the historical context of the CEBs' origins in Latin America in general, and then turn to their emergence in Mexico.

Context in Latin America at the Time of the Emergence of the CEBs

The CEBs were born in the midst of the Latin American struggle for greater equality in the Latin American society. Enrique Dussell, an Argentinean church historian currently teaching at the National Autonomous University of Mexico, argues that the Latin American church has passed through three main stages: colonial Christendom (1492–1808), Christendom in crisis (1808–1950) and the church of the common people (emerging gradually after 1950). The ecclesial transition has followed economic and political forces from a dependent colony of Spain and Portugal to the industrial revolution to neo-liberal capitalism.[1] The CEBs emerge from this history and are also a product of the socio-economic conditions of their time. In 1975 there were 110 million people living in poverty across Latin America. Today this figure has increased to 152 million.[2] This means that thirty-five percent of the total households in Latin America were living in poverty in 1980. Rather than decreasing, this figure has continued to grow.[3] The infant mortality rate throughout Latin America from 1980–1985 was 58.3 deaths for every 1,000 live births. In 1980 one in every five Latin Americans did not know how to read.[4] In this climate of poverty and injustice, liberation theology and the CEBs were born as a critical reflection upon the ongoing struggle against inequality.

These injustices in Latin American society led to unstable political climates. In the context of the cold war, military regimes throughout Latin America, often with the knowledge and support of the U.S. Central Intelligence Agency, overthrew democratic governments under the pretext of impeding communism. The general goals of the military coups were to stop subversion, and to promote development and national security. The military interventions with U.S. involvement in the 1960s and 1970s in Latin America include:

- February 29, 1954: CIA *coup d'état* "Operation WASHTUB" removed Guatemalan President Jacob Arbenz Guzman from office

- March 31, 1964: *Coup d'état* in Brazil with CIA involvement

- April 24, 1965: Juan Bosch's rebellion in the Dominican Republic put down by 23,000 American troops

- August 21, 1971: *Coup d'état* in Bolivia with CIA involvement

- June 27, 1973: Dissolution of the Uruguayan Congress

1. Dussell, "Current Events in Latin America (1972–1980)," in Torres and Eagleson, *Challenge of Basic Christian Communities*, 77–78.

2. The United States Agency for International Development. Online: http://qesdb.cdie.org

3. By 1997 36 percent of households in Latin America were living in poverty. Ibid.

4. The United States Agency for International Development, Indicators of Economic and Social Development in Latin America and the Caribbean. Online: http://www.eclac.01/publicaciones/Estadisticas

- September 11, 1973: *Coup d'état* in Chile with CIA involvement, overthrowing democratically elected Salvador Allende
- January 13, 1976: Fall of the nationalist military government in Ecuador
- March 24, 1976: Fall of Isabel Peron in Argentina

While these military interventions were an attempt to repress the popular left-wing movements in Latin America, the ensuing economic policies created more disparity between the rich and the poor.

The triumph of the Cuban Revolution in 1959 was in response to this disparity between the rich and the poor, but was a "red flag" for those who feared the advancement of communism in the Western Hemisphere. The response of President John F. Kennedy to such widespread poverty and the threat of popular uprisings was the "Alliance for Progress." This plan grew out of the paradigm of development, namely, if the West could build up the infrastructure (transportation, education, health care and energy sources) of Third World nations, they would then be able to compete in world capitalism and would not turn to communism.[5]

In order for democracy to work, the "Alliance for Progress" stipulated, the people must be trained, educated, healthy and have steady employment. Therefore, roads, schools, hospitals and energy plants were to be built with grants from the United States Agency for International Development. The United Nations declared the 1950s to be the "decade of development." More often than not, however, corrupt military governments and dictators siphoned off funds, or hired close associates with exorbitant construction contracts. Other international agencies, such as the International Monetary Fund and the World Bank, also worked in the spirit of "developmentalism," offering loans to Third World nations. However these loans created a foreign debt for future generations to pay off at the expense of essential government services in the national budgets. In spite of its best intentions, the efforts of the "Alliance for Progress" aggravated the situation rather than making it better. In 1968 President Richard Nixon conceded that, seven years after

5. Melendez, *Seeds of Promise*, 58.

the inception of the Alliance for Progress, nutrition and food scarcity in Latin America had worsened.[6]

Meanwhile, Latin Americans were gaining consciousness of their own problems and how to resolve them. The workers began to organize and protest low wages and unfair working conditions. In the 1940s and 50s in Brazil, church lay workers organized spheres of action where Catholic workers and student movements could meet in the "safe space" of the church. Among grass-roots left-wing movements there was a rejection of the development model in favor of a more radical approach. The Western model of development was discredited due to the United States' intervention in Vietnam and its own internal racial divisions.[7] The Cuban model of independence became increasingly attractive to Latin America.[8]

Origins of the CEBs in Latin America

These grass-roots resistance groups in Brazil were the precursors of the CEBs. They fulfilled two specific needs in the Brazilian context. Initially, students, workers and peasants began to organize around issues of worker rights. Later, following the 1964 military coup, the people gathered in resistance to the military government. One early member of the CEBs recalls its origins from the grassroots:

> I don't know for sure when these ecclesial communities began. I think it was around 1950. But I do know that they came into being because something was needed for survival. The number of these communities grew after 1964 and 1968, after the military coup and the increasing repression in our country. The people felt stripped of their dignity, their culture, and the fruits of their labor. They were facing disintegration. The base-level communities represented survival space. They were a place for resisting domination. Moreover, the people realized that the organization of the church into dioceses, prelacies, and parishes did not suit their needs. As structures, they were too big. The base-level community solved this problem, becoming a place

---

6. Galeano, *Open Veins of Latin America*.

7. Meléndez, *Seeds of Promise*, 58.

8. Ibid., 59.

for reflection and debate, for religious celebrations, and for all sorts of activities by Christians.[9]

These isolated local groups emerged to meet specific needs in local parishes. While they pointed to a pattern of a widespread need throughout the Brazilian context, and Latin America in general, they were still not Base Ecclesial Communities as such.

In addition to political resistance, the shortage of clergy and need for a more intimate sense of community created a need for a smaller structure within the parish.[10] In large urban areas and isolated rural zones the ratio of clergy to laity was very low, thus leaving large sectors of the population without much contact with clergy or spiritual guidance. The size of these parishes was so large that the population did not have a sense of community. The Protestant concept of a congregation was foreign to the Roman Catholic experience in Latin America at that time.

On the official level strides were taken to respond to the pastoral needs of the Brazilian context. In 1952 the National Conference of Brazilian Bishops was formed, allowing for a concerted effort to minister to the needs of their population. Ten years later the Brazilian bishops published the "Emergency Plan," which outlined the specific pastoral needs of their nation. As an outgrowth of that plan, in what could be considered the official launching of the Ecclesial Base Communities, the Brazilian Church called for "basic communities" within the parish structure in a Joint Pastoral Plan (1965–1970).[11]

Therefore when the Ecclesial Base Communities were formed, they were part of a planned evangelization and formation that was initiated by pastoral agents. Marcello de Azevedo confirms that: ". . . the [CEBs] did not arise spontaneously out of the base, out of common people composing them. They were the result of the consciousness-raising activity of clergy and religious, who were helping people to see real elements of their life and historical situation."[12] In most cases, a priest or

9. Da Silva, "Personal Testimonies," in Torres and Eagleson, *Challenge of Basic Christian Communities*, 214–15.

10. The growth of evangelicalism is proportionate to the shortage of clergy or the clergy: laity ration. See Bowen, *Evangelism and Apostasy*, 56–57.

11. Azevedo, *Basic Ecclesial Communities in Brazil*, 28–29.

12. Ibid., 35.

religious arrived in a neighborhood and began training lay people and introducing the CEB's Bible study methodology. Of course, it must be clear that the emergence of such a pastoral plan occurred in the midst of dramatic social changes within the Brazilian context specifically and the Roman Catholic Church more generally.

The Second Vatican Council, which met over four years in Rome (1962–1965), was a watershed event, not only for the church in Latin America, but all over the world. The neo-Thomistic post-reformation theology that avoided the scientific and mathematical advances of modernity had finally been finally challenged as Pope John XXIII called for the first ecumenical council since Vatican I of 1869–70.[13] The opening of Catholic ecclesiology allowed the church to encounter modern secularized society.[14] Vatican II clarified that the Reign of God began with Jesus Christ, and the task of the church was to: "announce and establish the Reign of Christ and of God, in the midst of all peoples, and constitute the seed and the beginning of this Reign on earth."[15]

A new emphasis was given to history as the place where God is present, and in its midst, the church was sacrament and the people of God. In order to accomplish this role of the church, the laity would have to become more involved. The shortage of clergy, particularly in rural areas, forced the Roman Catholic Church to involve the laity in strategies for evangelization.[16] The second Vatican Council responded to this crisis with the following statement:

> The laity are called particularly to make present and operative the church in those places and conditions of life where she cannot be the salt of the earth unless through them. In this way all laity, by the same gifts which have been conferred to them, are converted into witnesses and live instruments of the mission of the Church "according to the measure of Christ's gift (Ef.4:7).[17]

---

13. Cunningham, "Vatican II," in Musser and Price, *New Handbook of Christian Theology*, 505.

14. Azevedo, *Basic Ecclesial Communities in Brazil*, 31–32.

15. "Dogmatic Constitution of the Church," 10.

16. Boff, *Church, Charism and Power*, 125.

17. "Dogmatic Constitution of the Church," 42.

The priesthood, instead of occupying a position of authority, was reinterpreted as a ministry of service.[18] The Council document goes on to outline five crucial changes that would facilitate the work of the CEBs:

1. The Council affirmed the importance of the laity taking an active role in the church.

2. It called all Catholics, not just the clergy, to be involved in creating a more just world. At the same time the bishops recognized that the causes for much of the misery and suffering in the world could be located in human sinfulness.

3. The bishops insisted that all Catholics, clergy and laity alike, become more aware of the Scriptures.

4. The bishops called for a careful reading of the "signs of the times," which became the basis for the kind of "bottom-up" theology that has become characteristic of liberation theology and the base communities.

5. The Council set a tone that called for renewal and updating. What resulted was a sense of introspection and self-analysis that flowed into each of the specific documents. This tone also flowed into the church itself in the years that followed. Within this context, church leaders began to question the effectiveness of impersonal parish life and looked for other, more personal structures of church life.[19]

Vatican II's opening towards greater participation of laity in the congregational life of the Roman Catholic Church was a catalyst for the emergence of the CEBs.

Vatican II had paramount implications for the Latin American church. The subsequent meetings of the Latin America bishops, the emergence of the CEBs and the ensuing liberation theology were all made possible through Vatican II. Don Sergio Mendez Arceo, bishop of the Cuernavaca Diocese, was a key figure in the significant transformation of the Latin American bishops. He participated in the first Council of Latin American Bishops in Rio de Janeiro in 1955 and also had twenty-three interventions at the Second Vatican Council, particu-

18. Meléndez, *Seeds of Promise*, 57.

19. *Documentos Completos del Vaticano II*.

larly in the area of liturgy.[20] He comments on the significance of Vatican II in the development of the Latin American church:

> Yes, everything proceeds from Vatican II. I participated in the process that Vatican II has meant, above all in the relations with the world. Medellin was born there. Puebla was born there. This is to say that the process of Latin American liberation originates in Vatican II, without thinking in this way, without its roots, the basis of which is the Vatican II, one would not have been able to think of the later developments.[21]

While the changes in the Roman Catholic Church opened the door for formal organization of the CEBs, the Brazilians had already paved the way at the grass-root level. One of the concrete opportunities for lay participation after the Second Vatican Council was "Delegates of the Word."[22] This program trained laity to prepare a liturgy of mass or a celebration of the Word in the absence of a priest. One Delegate of the Word in Chile explains his ministry: "I lead the liturgy of the Word on Sundays when there is no mass. I teach catechism, celebrate baptisms and marriages; receive those who want to talk to me about their problems, visit those who no longer come to our meetings."[23] The Delegates of the Word is an innovative, powerful movement that reflects the spirit of lay participation from Vatican II.

In 1966 Base Ecclesial Communities also began in Panama and Nicaragua. A young Spanish priest teaching at the seminary in Managua requested permission from the bishop to develop a parish in a newly developed residential neighborhood. José de la Jara began the San Pablo Apóstol parish and developed a pilot project for pastoral care involving smaller community groups, the participation of the laity and a parish council. That same year Father Feliz Jimenez moved from the San Miguelito parish in Panama to San Pablo Apóstol Parish in Managua. He began to organize CEBs based on the Panama model of Bible studies with small groups of young couples and even organized a group from the San Pablo Apostle parish to visit San Miguelito in Panama.[24]

20. Chávez and Girardi, *Don Sergio Méndez Arceo*, 30.
21. Ibid.
22. Also known as "Ministers of the Word" in some countries.
23. Bavarel, *New Communities, New Ministries*, 50.
24. Mulligan, *Nicaraguan Church and the Revolution*, 91.

Also in 1966, Jesuit Priest Ernesto Cardenal was convinced by Father José de la Jara to not just preach the gospel, but rather to facilitate a discussion of the Word. Ernesto Cardinal began doing this in his parish on the Island of Solentiname with great success and founded a CEB.[25] These Bible studies were later transcribed into a four volume series entitled *The Gospel of Solentiname*.[26]

The CEBs spread from Brazil, Chile, Panama, and Nicaragua to other Latin American countries. CELAM, the Latin American Episcopal Conference, was a relatively new organization with the first meeting having taken place in Rio de Janeiro in 1955. The second meeting, known as CELAM II, was held in Medellin in 1968, and interpreted the events of the Second Vatican Council in light of the Latin American reality.[27] Vatican II's openness toward non-western interpretations of the gospel allowed the bishops at Medellin to move from being "an extension of a European church and [take] on its own identity."[28] For example, this conference recognized the extreme poverty that the majority of Latin Americans were suffering. Sociological tools were employed to reveal the structural injustice that institutionalized violence and oppressed the poor.[29]

As the church examined its role in society it discovered that the church is an integral part of the very social organization which established injustice and generated poverty and oppression and that the church, through its members, methods and institutions, continued to perpetuate the same conditions.[30] As a majority of its parishioners were urban and rural poor, the bishops in Medellin advocated social reform in the conclusion of their final document.[31] The Latin American church made a "preferential option for the poor" at the Medellin meeting in 1968 and ratified this stance at the next meeting of CELAM in Puebla in 1979.[32] At the same meeting in Puebla the Council of Latin American

25. Ibid., 89–90.

26. Cardenal, *Gospel of Solentiname*.

27. "Universidad Centroamericana," in *Documentos de Medellín*, 25.

28. Berryman, "CELAM II," in Musser and Price, *New Handbook of Christian Theology*, 78.

29. Azevedo, *Basic Ecclesial Communities in Brazil*, 36.

30. Ibid.

31. "Universidad Centroamericana," in *Documentos de Medellín*, 25.

32. MacEoin and Riley, *Puebla*, 91. Also see Boff and Boff, *Introducing Liberation Theology*, 46.

Bishops affirmed and celebrated the Ecclesial Base Communities as a new model of evangelization among the poor.

The growth of the CEBs in Latin America did not come without opposition. Between the meeting at Medellin and the next meeting in Puebla there was an attempt by more conservative forces within the church to counter the changes. For example, Bishop Sergio Mendez Arceo, who by this time was well known as an advocate of the CEBs and radical social change, was not invited to Puebla. In addition, the general secretary of CELAM, conservative Bishop Lopez Trujillo of Colombia, attempted to influence the agenda before the Puebla meeting by omitting any mention of the Ecclesial Base Communities from the preliminary document.[33] But the popular support and witness of the CEBs were too widespread, so that the final document of Puebla referred to the CEBs as a "reason for joy and hope" and as "centers of evangelization and moving forces of liberation."[34] The official statements in support of the CEBs at Medellin and Puebla marked the approval of the church hierarchy for a grass-roots movement that was already strong in Brazil, Chile, Panama, Nicaragua, and Mexico, in addition to other Latin American countries.

Organizational Structure of the Ecclesial Base Communities

What exactly is a CEB? A CEB is a small neighborhood-based Bible study group that reflects on one's reality in the light of Scripture. The heart of the Bible study is dialogue and discussion about the meaning of the passage in the lives of the participants. After identifying the problems in the neighborhood, the community reflects upon an appropriate course of action to solve those problems through the inspiration of the Gospel. In Church, Charism and Power (1985), Leonardo Boff indicates that the CEBs in Brazil are comprised of fifteen to twenty families who gather once or twice a week to study the Bible, worship, and share their common problems. Other reports in different settings have described smaller groups, but the concept of developing a small reflection group is the same.

33. Ibid., 39.

34. *Los Documentos de Puebla*, 96, 262, 1309.

One may be tempted to discard the CEBs as a traditional Bible Study. A closer look at the changes in the Roman Catholic Church after Vatican II shows a basic distinction. The Second Vatican Council was the Catholic Church's acknowledgement of the challenges of modernity, particularly an openness to dialogue with the sciences. The Second Vatican Council marked a transition from a deductive theology "from above" to an inductive theology "from below."[35] Dialogical theology forced the church to acknowledge experience as a valid source along with the orthodox sources of Scripture and tradition.

Given the opening to the authority of experience as a source for theology, the CEB methodology begins with *to see*, and continues with *to judge* and *to act*. More recently two other steps, *to celebrate* and *to evaluate*, were added to make a total of five methodological steps. The method of the CEBs begins with *to see* because the CEBs encourage their members to observe their reality, the injustices of society, in light of the gospel. The goal of this initial stage is that the participants identify or name their economic, political and ideological life circumstances. Father Javier Saravia, a Mexican Jesuit priest, utilizes the image of a "social tree" to describe the first step of the method. The roots represent the economic reality, the trunk the political reality and the branches the cultural reality.[36] Saravia then positions these three categories in relation to four sub-categories: 1) the needs of the people, 2) the resources available to the people, 3) the problems the people face and 4) the actions which cause or resolve the problems.[37] The result is a grid of twelve squares which represents the "social tree."

In the second stage, *to judge*, the participants of the CEBs are called to systematically analyze their reality. They diagnose the situation, judge what is good and bad in it, and identify the causes of the bad and its possible consequences.[38] For example, a CEB may struggle with an investor who buys a plot of land in the community to build a fast-food restaurant. Utilizing the "social tree" developed in the *to see* stage, the participants organize and prioritize the data.[39] One may ask ques-

35. Libanio and Murad, *Introducción a la Teología*, 96.
36. Saravia, *La Biblia*, 62.
37. Saravia, *Comunidades en Camino*, 38–39.
38. Ibid.
39. Boff and Boff, *Introducing Liberation Theology*, 87.

tions such as: Who *does* these actions and with what intention? What are the actions doing: exploiting or serving the people? Who benefits from these actions? *To judge*, is the bridge between *to see* and *to act*. This bridge rests on the pillars of the social sciences and the Word of God. These pillars with which the participants think help them to discover the beams of the bridge: judgment and solution.[40] The social sciences, for example Marxist economic theory, become a helpful instrument in analyzing systemic problems in society, such as the effect of fast-food restaurants on marginal communities.[41] Saravia utilizes the theory of structural social analysis to introduce the participants into the cause-and-effect relationship of the data.[42]

Then, using the Word of God, the participant identifies today's actors in biblical passages. For example, who are the Pharisees of today? Who is Pilate? One looks for the meaning of the Word of God in today's context.[43] The CEBs' methodology does not simply accept this reality as static; rather one judges it with a critical eye to determine the root causes of the injustice.

The third stage is *to act*. The whole purpose behind *to see* and *to think* is to get to the action: "It is a transformative action that changes the seen reality, according to what we have thought, to something better."[44] This stage leaves the strategy up to the group or context with the guideline that all action have an objective. This action is where the gospel is applied to reality. So the CEB, for example, may choose an action to respond to the threat of a fast-food restaurant in the community. Based on biblical models of action and liberation, one chooses an action to transform injustice. Saravia divides *to act* into five areas:

1. Evangelization: Evangelization is the action of communicating the Good News. . . . For the poor the announcing and realization of the Kingdom of God (justice, peace and truth in order to live a life of love) is good news.

2. Conscientization: Conscientization is the act of awakening the conscience so that people can recognize and comprehend reality.

40. Saravia, *Comunidades en Camino*, 63.

41. Boff and Boff, *Introducing Liberation Theology*, 28.

42. Ibid., 87.

43. Saravia, *Comunidades en Camino*, 63.

44. Ibid., 64.

It removes the blindfold that prevents people from seeing and understanding what is happening.

3. Organization: Organization is the act of integrating and organizing people into shared work. In order to advance more in this work, evangelization and conscientization are not enough because we cannot remain in the realm of words. The desire to do good and to bring about change is not enough.

4. Politicization: Politicization is the act of struggling to maintain power in the hands of the people.

5. Mobilization: Mobilization is the act through which the people work together and bring about their liberation in a total, comprehensive manner.[45]

Saravia's model encourages the group to begin with small tasks, but at the same time the methodology of the CEBs encourages its members to go beyond "band-aid" material assistance to the poor and attack root causes. This is also a reaction against the developmental model that has tried to reform the system from within.[46] Therefore the CEBs act, not only offering assistance to the poor, but also struggling against and seeking to transform the structural injustices of the system which continue to produce poverty.

After the initial revolutionary movements in the 1970s and 80s became long drawn out struggles, the CEBs realized that the struggle to build the Kingdom of God would be a long spiritual pilgrimage. Therefore the two additional steps of *to evaluate* and *to celebrate* were added to remind the CEBs to assess their actions and to celebrate along the journey.[47] *To evaluate* refers to the imperative to be self-critical and make mid-course adjustments in their strategy of social change. To implement this step, the national *encuentros* every four years in Mexico have produced national priorities which recognize shortcomings of the CEBs.

The final stage of the method is *to celebrate*. This is a favorite of the CEB gatherings because they often end with a time of fellowship

---

45. Ibid., 113–15.

46. Boff and Boff, *Introducing Liberation Theology*, 5.

47. For more discussion on self-criticism of the CEBs see Marins and Trevisan, *Las CEBs Siguen Bien, Gracias*, 68.

and refreshments. Since they tend to be very patriotic, they hold special celebrations with music and dancing to commemorate national holidays and historical dates. The CEBs also celebrate the national culture with music, dance and song. As the Brazilian saying "*A luta continua*" suggests, the struggle will continue and the members need to be spiritually and physically replenished. This last stage comes out of the CEB theology which recognizes the pilgrimage of the church which is on a journey toward liberation. Therefore the participants need *to celebrate* in the midst of the struggle and gain a sense of encouragement by mutually supporting one another in community.

The local units of CEBs are usually part of a parish or larger organization that is coordinated by a priest or an overseeing committee. This is indicative of the CEB ecclesiology of not being a separate parallel church, rather an alternative model of being the church.[48] This CEB overseeing committee in the diocese designs a curriculum of Bible studies and coordinates activities. Each local CEB selects, or is assigned, one *animador* or *coordinador*[49] to facilitate the Bible studies. The lay *animador* is trained through spiritual retreats and a weekly planning meeting. This meeting is a source of support, information and training for the *animadores,* during which, they receive lesson plans, instructions and announcements of upcoming events. This information, in turn, is reported back to the local unit of CEB. One parish that I visited in Mexico City divides the geographical area of the parish into sixteen local units of CEBs. In an interview with the priest, he showed me a large hand-drawn map of his parish where the boundaries of the local units of CEBs were neatly laid out. In Managua, the CEB's work is spread out in twenty-three neighborhoods in different parishes throughout the city. Some parishes, depending on the priest, support the work of CEBs in their midst, while others ignore or are hostile toward the CEB leadership. The continuing work in the face of resistance from the Catholic hierarchy depends on the commitment of the lay leadership and the strength and consistency of the organizational structure. For religious festivals, anniversaries, and other important occasions, all the local units are convened for a large celebration of worship and fellowship.

48. Ibid., 68.

49. In Mexico this lay facilitator is called an *animador*; in Nicaragua *coordinador*. This is a volunteer who is usually selected by the local priest with the support of the CEB constituency.

Vatican II's emphasis upon church as sacrament and people of God allows for a new interpretation of ecclesiology. Brazilian liberation theologian Leonardo Boff reflects upon the new ecclesiology of the CEBs in his appropriately titled book *Ecclesiogenesis:*

> We are not dealing with the expansion of an existing ecclesiastical system, rotating on a sacramental, clerical axis, but with the emergence of another form of being church, rotating on the axis of the word and laity. We may well anticipate that, from this movement, of which the universal church is becoming aware, a new type of institutional presence of Christianity in the world may now come into being.[50]

This new participatory and less hierarchical model fits well in the communal Latin American culture. As lay people participate in the Bible studies they become *conscientized*[51] and empowered to change the injustices around them. They relate their faith to the reality of their life conditions.

Development of CEBs in Mexico

The history of the CEB in each country is varied, however the emergence of the CEBs in Mexico can be traced directly back to one man. Bishop Sergio Méndez Arceo supported the emergence and growth of CEBs in his diocese of Cuernavaca. Aware of the lack of Bibles, Bishop Mendez Arceo initiated a project to distribute the Bible within the diocese in 1959. Without objection from Pope John XXIII, he promoted the use of the Protestant Bible because it was cheaper and translated into easier-to-read Spanish.[52] This move was particularly bold due to the antagonist Catholic-Protestant relations before Vatican II. Then during the Council, Bishop Méndez Arceo backed up his actions with numerous interventions to promote the vernacular use of the Bible.[53] Upon reaching his twenty-fifth anniversary as bishop in 1962, a book was compiled for the occasion which celebrated the accomplishment of

---

50. Boff, *Ecclesiogenesis*, 2.

51. "Conscientized" is an English adaptation from the Portuguese "*conscientizaciao*" which involves teaching people how to read while also raising awareness about the unjust structures in society. See Freire, *Pedagogy of the Oppressed*.

52. Arceo, "Recuperando la Memoria de 'Don Sergio Méndez Arceo,'" 36.

53. Rentaría, *Don Sergio Méndez Arceo*, 30.

the distribution of 10,000 Bibles and 30,000 New Testaments in his dio-cese.[54] Under the leadership of Bishop Méndez Arceo, Father Rogelio Orozco, a long-time priest in Cuautla and later in the parish of San Anton, developed traditional Bible studies from 1962–1968 to encour-age parishioners to develop greater knowledge of the Bible. These bibli-cal reflection groups were a precursor to the CEBs which would begin with the introduction of the CEB methodology under the leadership of two French priests.[55]

Father Pierre Rolland, a native of France, had been a volunteer missionary in Chile until 1966 when he left to begin a new mission in Cuba. But while traveling in Mexico he learned that he could not obtain a Cuban visa, so instead requested permission from Bishop Méndez Arceo to work as a priest in the diocese of Cuernavaca. The permission was granted and Rolland moved into a house in the work-ing class neighborhood of Carolina. Father Rolland had worked with base communities in Santiago, Chile, and soon he began developing them within the Mexican parish. In 1967 he recruited a number of married couples who would meet with him once a week to form their community. A hallmark of Rolland's work is that he always insisted on married couples, demanding the equal involvement of husbands and wives. He was trying to break the cultural stereotype that religion was a woman's domain. Founding members of the CEB still remember how Father Rolland visited the poor on his bicycle and encouraged them to think critically about their reality.

In 1968 Luis Genoel, another French priest who had worked with the CEBs in Chile, came to Cuernavaca. Genoel left Chile with the idea of going to India to work as a missionary, and just as Rolland, he came to Mexico to wait for his visa, but suffered the same fate of his country-man. So Bishop Méndez Arceo welcomed him to stay and assigned him to the parish of Teopanzolco. In the 1960s Teopanzolco was a working-class community on the eastern side of Cuernavaca, where the main source of employment was *Textiles Morelos*, a subsidiary of U.S.-owned Burlington Coat Factory. The wages were low, but the employees did not complain; instead they had an affectionate relationship with the

54. Diocese of Cuernavaca, *Don Sergio, 25 Años de Obispo*, 33.

55. Sánchez, "Don Sergio Méndez Arceo," in Chávez and Girardi, *Don Sergio Mén-dez Arceo*, 116.

Patron.[56] The *patrón* was a Frenchman who was a prominent figure in the community and many of the employees had his portrait on their living-room wall. He was Catholic like his workers and gave them gifts on important occasions and visited them when they were sick, yet their situation was dire. Yet, the people did not have a critical consciousness to question their living conditions.

Upon Father Genoel's arrival, he began organizing Bible study reflection groups, as had Father Orozco. However Father Genoel had read about the affirmation of the CEBs in the final conclusions of the Medellin Conference of Latin American bishops (CELAM, 1968), and as a result, he introduced the method (*to see, to judge, to act*) through Bible studies in a community setting. In addition to "*El Método,*" Genoel added another element not present in Orozco's earlier Bible studies—a persistence with one group over a year's time, which added the ingredient of community building. Initially the themes of his work with married couples were traditional Catholic catechism: Eucharist, matrimony, Scripture, theology, and morality. However, after observing that the social structure left people highly indebted to the *patrón* he began to introduce critical thinking into the process. Fr. Genoel recalls:

> Look at yourselves! You are all unaware that your religion is a religion of submission to the *patrón,* your belief is in the *patrón.* This is not Christian. I didn't have anything against this man. I knew him; we spoke French together. But this man enslaved the people.[57]

Father Genoel's methodology gradually led to a greater critical consciousness among his parishioners allowing them to reflect upon their reality.

Eventually the workers of the textiles organized and had a strike to protest working conditions. Several of the workers, including the family members of the participants of the CEBs, were jailed by the police. After speaking with the owner, Bishop Méndez Arceo came to visit the workers in jail. One of the organizers recalls:

> Twenty-four hours after being detained they announced that we had a visitor: Bishop Sergio Méndez Arceo. We were all

56. See above, 20 n. 49, for an explanation on the Spanish word *patron.*

57. Interview with Luis Genoel, August 7, 1989. See Emge, "Critical Thinking within a Religious Context," 35.

surprised to think that we were deserving enough for a person of that category to visit us in jail . . . We spent two hours explaining the multiple problems and humiliations that we were enduring.[58]

Bishop Méndez Arceo listened to the workers and took up their cause against unfair working conditions. As the methodology of the CEBs called for critical reflection of reality, the Christians joined with the workers' movement to seek justice.

Bishop Méndez Arceo was forced to retire in April of 1983, but not without leaving a thriving network of CEBs in his diocese for the remainder of the decade. The CEBs were clearly identified with liberation theology, provoking a strong reaction from the Roman Catholic hierarchy which stunted the growth of the CEBs: "The communities do not develop anymore; rather they simply maintain themselves at the current level. . . . In several cases, previously they were growing or prosperous, but the change of circumstances (principally the change of bishops and priests) made them shrink."[59] The antagonism that the CEBs faced in several parishes left their lay leaders alone and isolated from resources.[60] The 1990s would bring about a changing world climate which would cause a decline in CEB growth.

Another factor in the crisis of the CEBs was the change in the international political scene. Beginning with the Soviet internal reforms of *Glasnost* and *Perestroika* in the mid-1980s, the Eastern European socialist bloc began to crumble. In November 1989 the Berlin Wall fell and in August of 1991 the Soviet Union experienced an internal *coup d'état*. Seeing the changing political climate, leftist movements in Central America opted for peace accords and amnesty rather than continuing an uphill struggle against growing U.S. hegemony in the hemisphere. Closely identified with these movements, liberation theologians and leaders of the CEBs were isolated and criticized, thus presenting a challenge to the CEBs.[61]

---

58. Testimony of Gabriel Muñoz, October 28, 1999; my translation. Also see Sánchez, "Don Sergio Méndez Arceo, Obispo de Cuernavaca," in Chávez and Girardi, *Don Sergio Méndez Arceo*, 117.

59. Mier, *Las Comunidades Eclesiales de Base*, 133–34.

60. Otero, Fernández, and Guzmán, "Investigación de Autodiagnóstico," 92.

61. Ibid., 88.

These and other factors have stagnated CEB growth throughout Latin America—including Mexico—during the last fifteen years.[62] The changing political and ecclesial situation has left the CEBs uncertain about their place and identity. This has pushed the national coordinating office of the CEBs in Mexico to publish a document entitled: "National Challenges 2000–2004," which summarizes the CEB's top five priorities as determined by the delegates of the national *Encuentro* in October of 2000:

1. Strengthening the identity, vision and mission of the CEBs as an expression of the Church of the Poor, and responding to the Trinitarian God who invites us to live in community before the new reality of a neo-liberal, plural Mexico in the process of change and to be a sign of hope for an alternative lifestyle.

2. Emerging subjects. Empowering the leadership of women and gender equality, promoting the participation of young people, building solidarity with migrants, and respecting of indigenous rights and cultures.

3. Encouraging the consciousness and participation of citizens for a stronger civil society as a means of building the Kingdom of God.

4. Articulation: improving organizational structures and communication among isolated local units.

5. Alternative Projects: initiating and strengthening existing social assistance programs for the poor.[63]

This document was published as part of the effort by the CEBs to unify and strengthen their identity and purpose in light of the lack of support from the Roman Catholic hierarchy. As a result of this and other initiatives, the infrastructure and participation in existing communities have been maintained for the most part.

Analysis of the CEBs

By the time Gustavo Gutierrez's watershed book, *A Theology of Liberation*, was published in 1971, the Ecclesial Base Community move-

62. Ibid., 93.
63. "Retos Nacionales 2000–2004," Tenayuca, No.350.

ment was already well established. The publication of this book, and its subsequent translation into English, was more for the benefit of the outside world than a defining theology for the CEBs. Since the theology of the CEBs is a reflection upon liberating action, theology came afterwards. In other words, liberation theology begins with action followed by reflection and more action. Juan Luis Segundo calls this the hermeneutical circle.[64]

This hermeneutical circle de-constructs traditional theology in light of the Latin American reality. Segundo defines the hermeneutical circle as "the continuous changes of our present reality, both individual and social." He goes on to say that ". . . the circular character of each interpretation works in such a way that each new reality requires a new interpretation of God, which, in turn, changes reality, and so one must interpret again . . . continuously."[65] Segundo appropriates the concept of the hermeneutical circle from Rudolph Bultmann, who borrowed the tools from the nineteenth century masters of suspicion, Marx, Freud and Nietzsche, and adapted this hermeneutic to the Latin American theology. Segundo suggests that one ask basic questions about commonly accepted conceptualizations of life, forcing us to change our understanding of life, death, society, politics, and the world in general. Only such a change, or at least a suspicion about our inherited ideas and judgments, can allow theology to involve itself with reality and develop new more pertinent questions.[66]

Liberation theology[67] involves an interdisciplinary approach that utilizes several different tools of analysis. As it begins with a specific historical context, liberation theology appropriates history, philosophy, economics and other social sciences as tools of analysis. The social sciences are crucial for self-reflection upon the human project and helps analyze the difference between the "is" and the "ought to be."[68]

The incorporation of history into theology, is one of the contributions of liberation theology. Salvation occurs in the temporal and not

64. Segundo, *La Liberación de la Teología*, 13.

65. Ibid.

66. Ibid., 13.

67. While references in this study to liberation theology generally mean Latin American liberation theology, it is readily acknowledged that many oppressed peoples develop and utilize liberation theologies in their own struggles and contexts.

68. Ruether, *Liberation Theology*, 3.

in a separate "spiritual" time. God's revelation occurs in history through concrete interventions on behalf of the oppressed. In the Hegelian sense, God is working through history toward a liberation that will be consummated in the Reign of God. This occurs when injustice and sin are overcome through the building of a just society in history. For liberation theology, this will not occur in an abstract time and place; rather it will occur in human history here on earth.

As God's revelation occurs in history, liberation theology is called to the task of looking for "signs of the times." God has not only spoken through the Bible or within the church, but is also present and active in culture and contemporary history. The new pronouncements of Vatican II with regard to culture[69] allow Latin Americans to honor their folklore and see the work of God in their midst. As a result of Vatican II, the church becomes sacramental and honors the customs and peoples whom make up the body of Christ.

The CEBs have appropriated this doctrinal shift by affirming the typical dress, music and dance of their indigenous cultures. Popular religion, virgins and saints are also a source for doing theology. As a result, the experience of a people is validated and God speaks through culture. So people's experience as poor, suffering and oppressed is acceptable and influences how God's message is interpreted. Roman Catholic dogma and ecclesiology cannot be universally implemented because theology must begin with the local context. Liberation theology offers the important contribution of the collective experience and culture as sources for doing theology.

Liberation theology's belief in God also involves an ethical component. Philosophically, the relationship between faith and conduct is inherited from Immanuel Kant's moral imperative. One cannot have faith in God without a corresponding moral obligation for conduct here on earth. Like Kant, liberation theology rejects ritualistic religion ("pure religion") for its own sake, and only honors religious practices that move the believer to a more just lifestyle. Liberation theology's preferential option for the poor extends that obligation toward a struggle for liberation on behalf of the oppressed.

Faith for liberation theologians is not an individualistic pietistic faith, rather it is communitarian. Salvation is collective and is concretely

69. Meléndez, *Seeds of Promise*, 57.

actualized through more just and equal living conditions. Since salvation will occur in history through the construction of the Reign of God it is irrelevant to talk about individual salvation. According to liberation theology, the individualistic salvation which might occur in the after life is a myth which is convenient for the rich because it rewards a personalized faith which does not affect change in this world, thus favoring the status quo. This understanding of salvation is what provoked Marx to call religion "an opiate of the masses."

As in many other theologies, Scripture is a source of authority for liberation theology. Passages involving the intervention of God or God's preference for the poor are emphasized in the CEBs. Biblical figures such as Moses, the prophets and Jesus Christ are highlighted, particularly their critique of social injustice. Moses is the liberator from slavery and oppression who leads the people of God toward the promise land:

> I have observed the misery of my people who are in Egypt; I have heard their cry on account of their taskmasters. Indeed, I know their sufferings, and I have come down to deliver them from the Egyptians, and to bring them up out of that land to a good and broad land, a land flowing with milk and honey . . .[70]

The prophets condemned ancient Israel for its social sins and condemned the nation to judgment if it did not repent. For example the eighth century prophet Amos is recorded as having said: "For three transgressions of Judah, and for four, I will not revoke the punishment; because they sell the righteous for silver, and the needy for a pair of sandals they who trample the head of the poor into the dust of the earth, and push the afflicted out of the way . . ."[71]

In spite of the amount of attention dedicated to the liberation motif in the Old Testament, Jesus Christ is considered to be the primary model of liberator. In his book, *Jesus Christ Liberator*, Leonardo Boff stated: "He now goes ahead of us as way, light, symbol and archetype of the most integrated and perfect being."[72] His commitment to the inclusion of the poor, and his challenge to unjust structures are highlighted in New Testament passages such as Matt 19:23 where Jesus teaches that it is harder for a rich man to enter heaven than for a camel to go through the eye of a needle.

70. Exod 3:7–8.
71. Amos 2:6–7a.
72. Boff, *Jesus Christ Liberator*, 242.

Liberation theology starts with the reality of the poor and a commitment to address the structures which oppress them. It rejects reform or "developmentalism" as a model which only tinkers with the unjust social order, specifically neo-liberal economic policies. It goes beyond "band-aid" remedies and proposes a radical break from the present order to a model of liberation based on the gospel.

The CEBs were often repressed for being allies with revolutionary movements. This has been the price of being faithful disciples and carrying the cross of Jesus. As the above methodology indicates, the theology or reflection follows the liberating action of the people. Before they were even called CEBs, the church in Brazil was a place for the peasants and workers to organize and later to seek refuge from military repression. In Nicaragua the CEBs participated in the protests against the Somoza dictatorship and supported the Sandinista Revolution. In Mexico under the leadership of Bishop Sergio Méndez Arceo, the CEBs have been in solidarity with Central American revolutionary movements and provided refuge to exiles. The struggle on behalf of the oppressed has grown out of a commitment to the poor and an analysis of the social reality in light of the gospel.

Summary

In summary, the Ecclesial Base Community movement has developed in the context of the Latin American struggle against "developmentalism," military dictatorships and unequal distribution of wealth. The changes in the second Vatican Council opened the way for lay-led Bible study and reflection groups. The Latin American Council of Bishops (CELAM) met in Medellin (1968) and again in Puebla (1979) and in both meetings affirmed Ecclesial Base Communities as a new model of evangelism for the church. After their inception in Brazil, Chile, Peru and Central America, the CEBs arrived in Mexico under the auspices of Cuernavaca Bishop Sergio Méndez Arceo when French Priest Pierre Rolland brought the CEB method from Chile in 1966. Other priests and lay people organized several local units of CEBs in the Cuernavaca diocese and other parts of the country. The CEBs are small grass-roots reflection groups who draw guidance from the Bible to address their social reality. The groups differentiate themselves from other Bible study methods through the use of their unique methodology of *to see, to judge, to act, to evaluate and to celebrate* which calls for reflection upon action.

4

Comparison of Background Literature on Ecclesial Base Communities and Pentecostalism

Introduction

SCHOLARS IN THE FIELDS OF ANTHROPOLOGY AND SOCIOLOGY OF RE-ligion have published studies about the CEBs and Pentecostalism throughout Latin America, which provide valuable background information for my ethnographic research in Cuernavaca, Mexico. While I am not aware of another comparison study of these two movements carried out specifically in Mexico, the background literature based on previous studies in Brazil, Colombia, Chile and elsewhere do present certain parallels with my research. At the same time there are differences between these studies and this ethnographic study in Mexico. For one, the Mexican cultural and context is quite different from other Latin American countries—beginning with the devotion to the Virgin of Guadalupe. Another difference is that these previous studies, carried out in the fields of anthropology and sociology of religion, examined social and political phenomena, whereas my study in the field of theology focuses on how the CEBs and Pentecostalism relate to and impact the poor.

Three Comparative Studies: Rolim, Mariz, and Burdick

Brazilian sociologist of religion Francisco Cartaxo Rolim took an historical approach to the comparison of CEBs and Pentecostals. Concerned with both movements' participation in politics and social action, Rolim analyzed the history of Brazil's class struggle in the twentieth century. He found that CEBs in Brazil grew out of the already conscientized poor who had organized around working conditions and land reform under the umbrella of the Roman Catholic Church in the 1940s and 50s. He also found that early Pentecostalism had a social consciousness for these same reasons, until the North American missionaries brought a message of "disassociation" with the social and political reality.[1] Only later after the Roman Catholic Church began a persecution campaign against the Pentecostals did the latter gain a sense of identity as an oppressed people. Ironically, through this religious persecution, Rolim claims, the Pentecostals opened their minds to the issues of social injustice and gained a feeling of solidarity with oppressed social classes in Brazil.[2]

In the tradition of Emilio Willems, Rolim suggests that conversion is one way that Pentecostals publicly exhibit their protest against the traditional organization of society. For Pentecostals, conversion is a statement against both the Roman Catholic Church and the unequal balance of power in society. Cartaxo Rolim appropriates Willems' concept of symbolic protest:

> In Pentecostalism every believer is a direct and legitimate producer of his or her religious world. They thus defy not only the traditional way of doing religion, but the very structure of a classist society. Of course, this challenge is symbolic and not political.[3]

In spite of this symbolic protest against the traditional organization of society, Rolim observes that since their initial identification with peasant causes, most Pentecostals tend to stay out of politics. Therefore the Pentecostals' challenge to society, according to Rolim, does not move beyond the symbolic.

Unlike Pentecostalism, however, Rolim observes that the CEBs are more inclined to critical thinking with regard to the socio-political reality. The CEBs move beyond the verbal to concrete actions of social involvement: "The CEBs try, through social practices and reflection, to challenge imperialism and discover the causes of poverty of the lower classes and the social roots of this situation, as a result allowing

---

1. For more on the concept of separating political and spiritual realities, see Benjamin Gutierrez, *En La Fuerza del Espiritu*, 19.

2. Rolim, *Religião e Classes Populares*, 60–61. Also see *O Que e Pentecostalismo*, 73.

3. Ibid., 75; my translation.

its members to acquire a type of questioning religion."[4] Therefore the CEBs engage in both verbal reflection and social action to challenge the causes of social inequality. Thus, Rolim is clear that both movements, in spite of their different historical backgrounds, are working among the poor and have the potential for social action.

More recently Cecilia Mariz compared the two movements in northeastern Brazil. Her study does not deny that they have different values, but finds more commonalities than differences. Her research methodology, in line with the sociology of religion, involved reading secondary sources, interviews, life histories, observation of meetings and the literature produced by each group.[5] Although her purpose was not theological, her thesis touches on theology when she argues that the poor have beliefs and participation in small groups that help them cope with, or even escape from, poverty. This is where she finds common ground between the two movements:

> I do not deny that the ideal, verbalized values of Pentecostalism and the BECs differ in these ways [value elements], but I do criticize studies that focus primarily on the ideological elements of these movements and neglect the common experiences of their members.[6]

Mariz found that both CEBs and Pentecostalism offered effective tools for surviving the cruelty of poverty and possibly even overcoming it.

In order to cope with poverty, both movements believe in some type of conversion that questions the world in its current state. Mariz appropriates Berger and Luckman's concept of alternation[7] to argue that both CEBs and Pentecostalism break away from the traditional Roman Catholic religious orientation in Latin American society and participate in a conversion:

> Both Pentecostalism and the BEC require people to make choices to change the religious orientation they acquired by traditional means of socialization. Converts to either of these

---

4. Rolim as cited in Sepulveda, "Pentecostal Movement in Latin America," in Cook, *New Face of the Church*, 72.

5. Mariz, *Coping with Poverty*, 9.

6. Mariz, "Religion and Poverty in Brazil," in Cook, *New Faces of the Church*, 76.

7. Berger and Luckman, *Social Construction of Reality*, 196–97.

movements experience the limits of the conventional common-sense view of life and become critical of it.[8]

Mariz goes on to emphasize the importance of meeting in small groups as a sign of hope and encouragement for change. This decision to join a movement, and hence rebel against the status quo, rejects a fatalistic outlook on life and shows faith that their lives can be changed. In conclusion, Mariz argues that both groups have a similar impact upon the lives of their participants.

Another study of the CEBs and Pentecostals in Northeastern Brazil, by American anthropologist John Burdick, reached a very different conclusion. In his book entitled, *Looking for God in Brazil: The Progressive Catholic Church in Urban Brazil's Religious Arena*, Burdick describes four major differences between the two movements:

1. The members of CEBs are from more stable, financially well-off and literate segments of the working class population, while the Pentecostals tend to attract a broader segment of the working class poor.

2. Married women find it difficult to resolve domestic problems through the CEBs, meanwhile in the Pentecostal church they find a supportive atmosphere which recruits members on the basis of suffering.

3. Unmarried youth who are under social pressure for consumption and sexuality find that Pentecostalism encourages a clear break with the past, something they do not find in the CEBs.

4. And finally, Burdick argues that the CEBs do not offer an effective "counterdiscourse" to racism, which the Pentecostals provide through spirit possession.[9]

In sum, Burdick found that much of the material written about CEBs by liberation theologians did not correspond to the reality that he observed in local units. He found the Pentecostal churches to be more effective in creating a positive change in the lives of their members.

---

8. Mariz, "Religion and Poverty in Brazil," in Cook, *New Faces of the Church*, 77.
9. Burdick, *Looking for God in Brazil*.

Where Are the Poor?

A central question in my review of background literature has been to examine how these two movements have related to or impacted the poor. When I refer to the poor, I do not limit this definition to economic criteria. Rather I believe that class has economic, social, political and ethnic dimensions.[10] Miguel Concha observes:

> In fact, the notion of class is a sociological, scientific, and historical concept of great profundity and richness. When we talk about social class, we are not talking merely about the economic nature of groups. Neither should the economic realm be presented as something isolated and exclusive. Marx himself insisted that the economic level is the starting point for an analysis of society as a whole.[11]

As I compare and contrast literature written about the CEBs and Pentecostalism in Latin America, I will primarily focus on how each movement relates to and impacts the poor. While I begin with the economic level, social determinants like education will be examined to evaluate the impact of the two movements on the poor.

It has been noted that both groups work with the poor, however a close reading of studies of both movements reveals slight differences. The early sociological studies of Pentecostalism by Lalive d'Epinay and Willems have both concluded that: "Pentecostalism is a religion of the poor, that offers both psychological security and the minimal material security necessary to cope with a hostile environment."[12] Gamaliel Lugo asserts not only that popular Protestantism is constituted primarily of peasants, laborers, indigenous, students and unemployed, but also that the Pentecostal church is a place where the exploited are given strength to overcome their marginalization.[13] It must be noted, however, that while Pentecostalism in Latin America is predominantly a religion of the poor, there are different social classes represented within the move-

---

10. Concha, "Interpreting Situations of Domination," in Torres and Eagleson, *Challenge of Basic Christian Communities*, 59.

11. Ibid., 58.

12. Dodson, "Pentecostals, Politics and Public Space in Latin America," in Cleary and Stewart-Gambino, *Power, Politics, and Pentecostals in Latin America*, 26.

13. Lugo, "Ética Social Pentecostal," in Alvarez, *Pentecostalismo y Liberación*, 107. Also see d'Epinay, *Religión e Ideología* 52.

ment.[14] It is not uncommon to find middle-class or even upper-class Pentecostal congregations, but they do not usually mix with the prototype working-class congregation.

Although the CEBs have affirmed the "preferential option for the poor," as adopted at CELAM II in Puebla (1979), studies have revealed that their membership is more diverse. Liberation theologian Sebastian Mier has acknowledged that there are well-educated and economically well-off pastoral agents involved in the CEBs:

> Now, together with the majority of the poor persons, in the CEBs, we also find multiple pastoral agents who—although numerically few—carry out significant roles within the life of the CEBs. These pastoral agents are bishops, priests, religious and lay people, whom we cannot consider economically poor. They usually live modestly, but their personal, family and congregational economic resources and other social factors make them far from destitute. Many of these agents come from the middle-class and some are wealthy.[15]

Francisco Cartaxo Rolim had noticed these differences in his earlier examination of the CEBs, and also saw that the presence of persons of different classes produced subordination within the CEBs.[16] A January 2001 self-diagnosis of the CEBs in Mexico highlighted this ongoing concern: "This means that an organization located within the popular sector with a majority of poor people is still led by a minority sector of middle-class people."[17] The difference between these CEB pastoral agents and the middle-class Pentecostal congregations is that the pastoral agents affirm the preferential option for the poor and elect to offer their time and serve in a working-class *barrio* while the middle-class Pentecostals do not. Moreover, while some Pentecostals have no objection to opening a congregation in a middle-class neighborhood, but this would be unusual for the CEBs.

In spite of the CEB's motto of a "preferential option for the poor," Mier's examination of the members of the CEBs revealed that the most needy in the neighborhood did not participate:

14. Andre Droogers, "Visiones paradójicas sobre una religión paradójica," in Boudewijnse et al., *Algo Más Que Opio*, 27.

15. Mier, *Las Comunidades Eclesiales de Base*, 155–56; my translation.

16. Rolim, *Religiao e Clases Populares*, 96.

17. Otero, Fernández, and Guzmán, "Investigación de Autodiagnóstico," 77.

> They [members of CEBs] are poor, yes, of scarce resources, but with a certain level of solvency. The most needy for multiple reasons (among others, naturally their economic urgency) do not participate (cannot participate) in the activities that would result in a sub-division [of their resources] . . .[18]

While Mier dismisses the absence of the marginalized in terms of a lack of time, other observers have found the poor more widely present in non-Catholic churches.

The late liberation theologian Richard Shaull found this to be true in Brazil. After working with the CEBs in the early 1960s in Brazil he was forced to leave the country for twenty years during the military dictatorship. Upon returning in the mid-eighties he discovered that the impact of the global economy and Brazil's economic reforms had produced vast numbers of impoverished and marginalized people. Seeking areas where faith and biblical reflection could be signs of new life and hope, Shaull witnessed an unexpected phenomenon: the marginalized sectors were flocking to the Pentecostal movements at an extraordinary pace.[19] He explains: "Pentecostals address themselves primarily to those who are poor and marginal where they are—overwhelmed by the struggle for survival, in the face of the disintegration of personal and social life."[20] Thus, this review of background literature reveals that some of the most marginalized sectors of the population feel more attracted to Pentecostalism than to the CEBs. This general tendency varies greatly from country to country, since neither group is homogenous and there are exceptions in both movements. The next section will explore some possible explanations of this tendency.

Rational and Emotional Religion

The emphasis on reading the Bible in both the CEBs and Pentecostalism enables participants to develop literacy and communication skills. Both groups, in spite of using different methodologies, consider the Bible to be authoritative, Cecilia Mariz observed:

> The importance of the written word and the theoretical elaboration of the faith has, as a consequence, encouraged people to

18. Ibid.; my translation.

19. Shaull and Cesar, *Pentecostalism and the Future*, x.

20. Ibid., 89.

become literate for the purpose of reading the Bible and to develop speaking skills for expounding scripture and discussing it
with others. . . .[21]

In spite of the Pentecostal emphasis on the emotional aspect,
the oral word also adds a rational element that helps it to contribute
to democratization. Mariz suggests that the poor are not attracted to
Pentecostalism because of its magic, miracles and emotion. These elements are already present in popular religiosity and are part of the
worldview of the poor. Rather, the poor seek to develop the element
of rationalism, order and legitimacy inherited from Pentecostalism's
Protestant roots. Mariz's ideas are built upon Max Weber's findings in
The Protestant Ethic and the Spirit of Capitalism, namely that reason, as
acquired through religion, contributes toward the modernization and
development of society.[22] The poor seek the "relative rationalization"
which Pentecostalism offers. Mariz states ". . . Pentecostalism is still ra-
tionalizing, since it introduces a universal ethic and stresses individual
choice of religion, exclusivity of religious identity, and the construction
of a theoretical system that integrates religious beliefs."[23] While the
occasional observer of Pentecostal worship might find disorder and
chaos, close observation indicates order and reason. As Mariz found the
element of reason in both Pentecostalism and the CEBs, she went on to
argue, in the spirit of Weber, that a religious experience that substitutes
reason for myth helps equip the poor to solve their problems.[24]

Although reading skills were important in both groups, Burdick
found that the intellectual content of a CEB meeting made literacy a
barrier for participation:

> In such situations, illiterates depend on literates to read or at
> least explain the lesson to them. The readings are often complex,
> utilizing specialized vocabulary. For many members this vocab-
> ulary resembles, in its unintelligibility, the Latin pre-conciliary
> prayer.[25]

21. Mariz, "Religion and Poverty in Brazil," in Cook, *New Faces of the Church*, 77.

22. Weber, *Protestant Ethic and the Spirit of Capitalism*.

23. Mariz, *Coping with Poverty*, 8. Also see Howe, *Algo Más Que Opio*, 35 and
Alvarez, *Pentecostalismo y Liberación*, 91.

24. Mariz, *Coping with Poverty*, 8. Also see Shaull and Cesar, *Pentecostalism and the
Future*, 25.

25. Burdick, *Looking for God in Brazil*, 76–77 .

These intellectual skills could be a factor in the exclusion of the most marginalized sectors of the population whose culture is largely oral. One reason behind the more intellectual and written content of CEB meetings may be that its purpose is different. It is intended to be a Bible study reflection group with a specific methodology (*to see, to judge, to act, to celebrate* and *to evaluate*) designed to conscienticize the person toward political participation in the liberation of the oppressed. Although it involves prayer, liturgy and singing, its primary purpose is not worship.

The Pentecostal meeting, on the other hand, is a worship service. Even when the meeting takes place in a home, or the focus is Bible study, it is usually set within the context of worship. In spite of the difference of purpose in the meeting, scholars such as Burdick still argue that Pentecostalism requires less intellectual skill and places a greater emphasis on the oral medium as opposed to the written. The spoken word is the principal medium of communication in the Pentecostal worship service. Certainly the Bible is read, but there is no lesson plan or bulletin to guide the congregation. Brazilian sociologist Waldo Cesar explains:

> The word dominates the Pentecostal service. The pastor already has a microphone in his hand. Nobody escapes from the sound that the speakers distribute through the enormous space of the service. Orality, the maximum expression of worship, predominantly improvised, mobilizes those present.[26]

The oral medium is more spontaneous and less inhibiting than the written for the participant. The emphasis on the Holy Spirit in Pentecostal doctrine facilitates flexibility during worship. Spontaneity must take precedence over order to allow for the Holy Spirit to be free.

The Pentecostal emphasis on speaking in tongues[27] as initial evidence of the baptism of the Holy Spirit is an important aspect of the Pentecostal doctrine of the Holy Spirit. Cesar observes how glossolalia take on a deeper meaning: "For those who receive the gift of speaking in unknown tongues, the phenomenon means surpassing language itself,

26. Shaull and Cesar, *Pentecostalism and the Future*, 42.

27. The technical term is glossolalia, which comes from the Latin *glossa*, tongue and *lalia*, speak, and is defined as the religious phenomenon of making sounds that constitute, or resemble, a language not known to the speaker. For further discussion, see Burgess and McGee, *Dictionary of Pentecostal and Charismatic Movements*, 335.

creating, improvising, and living the ecstasy of an unspeakable grace."[28] Since this language is often unintelligible, a second gift of the Spirit is interpretation, which may be given to the same person or to a different individual. This is similar to the gift of prophecy, which authorizes a member to speak God's word directly to the congregation. Speaking in tongues, interpretation and prophecy are oral media through which God may communicate directly a message specifically related to the context of the participants. Although speaking in tongues is the initial evidence of baptism of the Holy Spirit, members must exhibit acceptable moral behavior in order to gain the authority to transmit a message to the congregation. Even denominations that prohibit women preachers still respect the ability of women to be used as prophets by the Holy Spirit. Regardless of gender, economic class or scholastic level, the Pentecostal doctrine of the Holy Spirit makes these oral forms of communication, and the authority attached to them, accessible to all.

Oral communication in Pentecostal worship has many similarities to the oral tradition of the *popular*[29] culture of the poor. The early studies of Cartaxo Rolim in Brazil revealed that the religious agents of Pentecostalism transmit their message to the masses through the medium of popular language, thus distinguishing themselves from the language of traditional Protestantism and Catholicism.[30] The reason for the use of popular language is that these religious agents are common people, coming from the same social surroundings, who give testimony to the Pentecostal experience.[31] By virtue of using common language, the word takes on a symbolic value that has meaning in the everyday lives of the participants.

Unlike the CEBs, Pentecostalism's emphasis upon the oral and the Holy Spirit opens a space for religious ecstasy. Just as the popular language speaks to the poor, Pentecostalism fulfills a need which many Latin Americans have for an emotional experience of communion with

28. Shaull and Cesar, *Pentecostalism and the Future*, 55. Also see Deiros and Mraida, *Latinoamérica en Llamas*, 67.

29. I have decided to retain the Spanish and Portuguese word *popular* in its native form. Therefore it is in italics to remind the reader to use its Latin definition as "base" or "grass roots."

30. Rolim, *Religiao e Clases Populares*, 140.

31. Sepúlveda, "El Crecimiento del Movimiento Pentecostal en América Latina," in Alvarez, *Pentecostalismo y Liberación*, 87.

the deity.[32] In the secular definition, ecstasy means an experience of "intense delight or loss of self-control during an intense experience."[33] However, religious ecstasy involves an encounter with the divine that takes on deeper meaning. Certainly the Pentecostals would reject any secular understanding of ecstasy or trance as diabolic. But on the practical level the Pentecostal finds great assurance from feeling the divine providence in life's everyday tasks:

> The [believer's] life is lived in constant allusion to divinity, an allusiveness filled with extraordinary intensity and excitement: upon arising the [believer] knows his or her day will not be ordinary, but will be filled with innumerable signs of God's carefully guiding hand.[34]

Pentecostal's ability to convert the mundane into significant faith experiences is attractive to the poor. This emotional intensity and excitement is not usually a part of the CEB experience.

Allard Westra appropriates Willems to argue that Pentecostalism is more compatible with *popular* religiosity[35] than the CEBs.[36] The *popular* beliefs in witchcraft and the spiritual realm are not reflected in the CEBs´ materialist analysis of society. Pentecostals, on the other hand, are in touch with the commonly held belief in the existence of demons and evil spirits. According to Willems, Pentecostals enter into a religious ecstasy and establish an emotional tie with the supernatural.[37] Jean-Pierre Bastian observes the similarities between the Pentecostal worship and *popular* Catholicism:

> The *popular* Pentecostal sermon is centered on the need to make the "forces of light" rise through "signs and wonders" that

32. Willems, *Followers of the New Faith*, 20.

33. *Microsoft Encarta Dictionary*, 279.

34. Burdick, *Looking for God in Brazil*, 63.

35. "Popular religiosity" depends greatly on the country and region in Latin America. The imposition of Roman Catholicism during the conquest often resulted in a syncretism with the native beliefs. In addition African religions were imported with the slaves and resulted in a new syncretism.

36. Allan Westra, "La conducta del consumidor en el mercado brasileño de salvación. La opinión pública relativa al Pentecostalismo y las religiones afro-americanas en la ciudad provincial de Alagoinhas (Bahía)." Boudewijnse et al., *Algo Más Que Opio*, 119. Also see Mariz, *Coping with Poverty*, 78.

37. Doogers, in Boudewijnse et al., *Algo Más Que Opio*, 47.

are manifested in glossolalia, taumaturgia and shamanism. The object of the popular Catholic and Pentecostal systems is in this sense identical, since they both try to negotiate with supernatural forces in which the faithful promise something in exchange for a blessing from God.[38]

Bastian goes on to argue that Pentecostals are more like rural Catholics without a priest than Protestants.[39]

The CEBs, however, criticize Pentecostals, and Protestants in general, for being a foreign importation. The case has been made that some evangelical sects have been sponsored by the religious right of the United States in accordance with foreign policy objectives.[40] Certainly, most Protestant denominations in Latin America have been planted by U.S. churches and, intentionally or unintentionally, carry with them an ideology. Yet today many Pentecostal denominations either are "fully indigenous churches" or have been able to shed their North American roots and adopt Latin American cultural forms. Recent research has highlighted Pentecostalism's ability to appropriate local language and symbols, at the same time that liberation theology has been criticized for using distant intellectual jargon.

> Liberation theology has a decidedly middle-class and radical intellectual accent alien to the localized needs of the "poor." . . . This means that while the language of Pentecostalism is 'odd' and many of its practices initially unattractive, the language of liberalism can easily remain remote.[41]

While liberation theology may use remote language that deals with idealized versions of reality, the CEBs are on the grass-roots level utilizing *popular* religiosity as a means of identifying with the people. The ability of Pentecostals to appropriate grass-root symbols and language gives them legitimacy and drawing power in the eyes of the poor. The similarities between Pentecostalism and *popular* symbols end, however, when the Pentecostals reject any icons, saints or images of the Virgin as idolatrous.

38. Bastian, *Protestantismos y Modernidad Latinoamericana*, 252; my translation.

39. Ibid., 282.

40. See discussion in chapter 2 on Diamond, *Spiritual Warfare*, and J. Samuel Escobar, "Conflict of Inter-pretations of Popular Protestantism," in Cook, *New Face of the Church in Latin America*.

41. Martin, *Tongues of Fire*, 290.

While it is common for the CEBs to utilize *popular* religiosity in their pilgrimages and worship of the Virgin, the focus of their meetings is more intellectual than emotional. They certainly appreciate *popular* religiosity as an opportunity to invite persons into the CEBs, yet once inside their group the methodology attempts to conscientize the individuals to grow towards a more intellectual and less superstitious understanding of their faith. Reflecting upon their reality in the light of the gospel, the CEBs utilize the human sciences to analyze unjust social structures. This systematic approach helps to identify the structural causes of injustice, responds with a prophetic voice and works for long-term solutions. However this methodology often has been perceived by the marginalized as a distant or idealized approach to their daily needs for survival.[42] Although the social analysis facilitated by the CEBs is necessary to raise consciousness about the systems which impoverish the poor, the rapid growth among the poor of Pentecostalism would appear to indicate that the marginalized prefer the immediate solutions offered by Pentecostalism.

Leadership Styles

How do the leadership styles in both movements foster or discourage democratization? Lalive D'Epinay and Bastian have argued that Pentecostalism is a re-creation of society in an attempt to reconstruct the *hacienda* structure with the pastor replacing the *patrón* as the dominant authoritarian figure. This kind of Pentecostal leadership style, according to Lalive d'Epinay and Bastian, discourages democratization.

In another interpretation of Pentecostalism's contribution to democracy, David Martin and other scholars appropriate Willems' work to dispute this position and claim that "conversion" is a believer's decision to break with the *status quo* and adopt an eschatological vision of an egalitarian society. These two diverging interpretations represent very different impressions of Pentecostal leadership styles. Mariz carves out a position between these major theories:

> It appears, however, that despite being as authoritarian as folk religions and popular culture as a whole, Pentecostalism fosters a different kind of authority legitimation. The authority of pastors in conferred not only by their personal charisma and style

42. Shaull and Cesar, *Pentecostalism and the Future*, 89.

but also by the institution they belong to and by their ethical behavior. Pastors must follow the "doctrine," or religious ethic; otherwise, church members may disobey them.[43]

Therefore, according to Mariz, although Pentecostalism does not imitate the same leadership patterns of traditional society, it is still largely authoritarian.

Mariz analyzes the leadership style of CEB *animadores* as being participatory, yet also reports instances of an authoritarian tendency in certain CEB leaders who dominate the decision-making process instead of listening to other people's opinions.[44] The design of CEB meetings is oriented toward small-group discussion in which the development of verbal skills is very important. This form of ecclesiology, in addition to its practical approach of being the church in the absence of priests, is also a critique of the hierarchical authoritarian style of the Roman Catholic Church.[45] Participation is strongly encouraged—although at first most poor people feel insecure about speaking in public. Mariz concludes that the CEB leadership style is a relative democracy.[46]

Martin concurs that the Base Communities are lay and "Protestant" in their form and style, but their ties to a hierarchical church limit the CEBs' autonomy and leadership style.[47] Similarly Burdick believes that in spite of the democratic intentions of CEB lay leaders, the power dynamic of the Roman Catholic hierarchy impedes a truly participatory decision-making process.[48] In addition the dependency upon literacy for participation in the CEBs creates a division between the literate and illiterate, thus impeding full participation.[49] The methodology of the CEBs is intended to foster more freedom, particularly political freedom, in Latin America; however the resistance of hierarchical authorities within the Roman Catholic Church has frustrated these efforts.[50]

The leadership style of Pentecostalism has been paradoxical. On the one hand it has an egalitarian vision of the Reign of God where all

43. Mariz, *Coping with Poverty*, 76.

44. *Ibid.*

45. Boff, *Ecclesiogenesis*, 24.

46. Ibid., 77.

47. Martin, *Tongues of Fire*, 286.

48. Burdick, *Looking for God in Brazil*, 44.

49. Ibid., 76–79.

50. Dodson, "Pentecostals, Politics, and Public Space in Latin America," in Cleary and Stewart-Gambino, *Power, Politics, and Pentecostals in Latin America*, 29.

people, regardless of their race, class, gender or educational level, will be full participants. On the other hand, it has the hierarchical tendencies of male-dominated authoritarian leadership styles.[51] While these tendencies appear to contradict each other, they are often operative simultaneously in the same church.[52] Leadership styles are varied within Pentecostalism, but more often than not its utopian vision of egalitarianism is not realized in the practice of its ecclesiology.

Small Groups and Empowerment

In spite of these differences in leadership style, both movements employ the method of small groups. Throughout church history beginning with the primitive church, small groups are found and reinvented at different historical times, for example in monasticism, Philip Jacob Spener's *ecclesiole en ecclesia*, Count Zinzendorf's Moravian bands and John Wesley's class meetings. The CEBs draw on this history, but have a unique methodology that differs from Protestant preoccupation with personal holiness.[53] Implemented in the aftermath of Vatican II's opening toward lay participation and liberation theology's call for reflection on the struggle for liberation, small groups conscienticize the laity for political participation in society.

Many Pentecostals also use small groups as a part of their ecclesiological structure. Similar to the CEBs, small groups are a method of evangelism that takes place in private homes in the neighborhood. The content of these meetings includes Bible study, prayer and worship. Their purpose is to reach people in the community who may be reluctant to physically attend a non-Catholic Church. Yet not all Pentecostal churches use small groups, due to the centralization of leadership and the fear of schism. The Pentecostal emphasis upon the Holy Spirit allows for prophets to be spontaneously called by God, and some pastors fear giving so much freedom to lay leaders.[54] It is not unusual in Pentecostalism for one of the cell groups, led by a leader, to rebel against the pastor and start one's own church. Sometimes these divisions oc-

51. Droogers, in Boudewijnse et al., *Algo Más Que Opio*, 37.

52. Westra, in Boudewijnse et al., *Algo Más Que Opio*, 131.

53. Cook, *New Face of the Church*, 355. Also see Bruno, "Ecclesiola in Ecclesia," 315–42.

54. Deiros and Mraida, *Latinoamérica en Llamas*, 230.

cur with the intention of starting new churches, but for the most part they result from a disagreement with the pastor. Waldo Cesar affirms that Pentecostal divisiveness reflects the overall Protestant tendency toward division.[55] These separations are also cited to justify the Catholic criticisms that these groups are merely sects. Scholars of Pentecostalism have also described these separations as a latent church growth strategy contributing to the empowerment of laity and the diversification of Latin American society.[56]

Each in its own way, the small groups of CEBs and Pentecostalism have the effect of building the self-esteem of its participants by encouraging literacy, developing verbal skills and providing a support network.[57] Although raising the self-esteem of participants is an effect of the CEBs, their methodology is less concerned with micro-psychological transformation than with systemic social change. This is apparent in their goal of conscientization as appropriated from the work of Brazilian pedagogue Paulo Freire.[58] It is based on a Marxist dialectical view of history that encourages the illiterate to learn to read while gaining an awareness of their reality as oppressed "objects" of history. The methodology critiques the traditional "banking" pedagogy that provides information to the student without empowerment. Freire's revolutionary method teaches literacy while empowering people to be "subjects" of history and thus participate in their own liberation. The CEBs accomplish this through their methodology of *to see, to judge, to act, to celebrate* and *to evaluate* that is based on the hermeneutical circle of reflecting on the struggle for liberation.[59] As this is accomplished participants gain self-esteem, awareness about their ability to work for the transformation of their reality, and empowerment to struggle for the liberation of their people.

The CEBs have criticized Pentecostalism for abandoning the interests of the working-class and deceiving its membership with false promises.[60] Recent literature on Pentecostalism has challenged this

55. Shaull and Cesar, *Pentecostalism and the Future*, 95.

56. Westra, in Boudewijnse et al., *Algo Más Que Opio*, 131.

57. Mariz, "Religion and Poverty in Brazil: A comparison of Catholic and Pentecostal communities," in Cook, *New Faces of the Church*, 81.

58. Freire, *Pedagogy of the Oppressed*.

59. Segundo, *Liberación de Teología*, 11.

60. Mariz, "El Pentecostalismo y el Enfrentamiento a la Pobreza en Brazil," in B. F. Gutiérrez, *En La Fuerza del Espíritu*, 199.

critique. Cheryl Bridges Johns, in her book, *Pentecostal Formation: A Pedagogy among the Oppressed*, disputes the stereotype that Pentecostals deny their historical existence and suggests that Pentecostals engage in conscientization. Citing Pentecostals' humble roots in Negro spirituals, millenarianism and the utopian vision of the Holiness movement, Johns encourages Pentecostals to draw upon this "corporate memory" and engage in the prophetic task of conscientization.[61] While one cannot deny that a relationship exists between Pentecostalism and conscientization, it remains to be seen how many Pentecostals will heed Johns' call to draw upon their "corporate memory" of early resistance.

The charismatic worship is another activity of Pentecostalism that constructs a sacred human dignity and empowers its participants to resist the forces of brokenness in their daily lives:

> Whatever its limitations, the Pentecostal message and experience had radically transformed [the poor's] understanding and experience of their world and enabled them to put together their broken lives and thus find new life and energy. Poor marginalized women and men had found the power they needed for physical, mental, and often material renewal and for a successful struggle to overcome the most destructive forces around them.[62]

Perhaps the language of Pentecostalism does not encourage a direct participation in politics or social problems, but the latent effect upon its membership is transformation. The spiritual experience of communion with the divine found in charismatic worship empowers the poor with the emotional and spiritual strength to meet life's daily challenge of survival.

Social Action and Politics

The leadership style, internal democracy and empowerment of the poor in both movements will eventually affect the members' participation in society, either as a manifest or latent effect. While the CEBs have often been accused of being too political, Pentecostalism has been criticized as being a private or apolitical religion. Yet each movement has a complex relationship to the public arena. Given the diversity and

61. Johns, *Pentecostal Formation*, 70.

62. Shaull and Cesar, *Pentecostalism and the Future*, 119.

complexity of both movements, it is difficult to arrive at any conclusive statements on each movement's relationship to political involvement. Early assessments of Pentecostal participation in politics were largely influenced by D'Epinay's paradigm of Pentecostalism's growth based on *anomie*. Any participation in society from this perspective was an attempt to reconstruct traditional authoritarian structures. More and more scholars such as David Martin have favored Willem's paradigm of Pentecostalism as a symbolic protest against traditional society. It is precisely the juxtaposition of the eschatological vision of an egalitarian society with the current corrupt order that calls Pentecostals to a radical egalitarian social ethic.

Pentecostal theologian Eldin Villafane has developed a Pentecostal social ethic which states that if one lives in the Spirit, there are ethical consequences calling one to participate in the historical project of the Reign of God.[63] He calls his theory an "ethic of pneumatology" which is based on the pillars of love and justice, and emerges from an experience in the Spirit. A corporate memory of resistance and the potential for symbolic protest against the current social order can be found in the Pentecostal tradition.

While the Pentecostals have a potential for political involvement, the CEBs have a proven track record of challenging injustice. In Brazil the CEBs emerged from an involvement in national student and workers' movements.[64] In Nicaragua in the 1970s the Base Communities participated in public demonstrations against the Somoza dictatorship and some of its youth joined the Sandinista revolution.[65] Workers' strikes in the early 1970s at the textile factories in Cuernavaca resulted in several of its leaders being jailed. The CEBs, led by Bishop Mendez Arceo, intervened on behalf of the rights of the workers.[66] The influx of Chilean refugees to Cuernavaca after the 1972 *coup d'état* and the revolutionary movements in Central America motivated to read Bishop Méndez Arceo and the CEBs to be in solidarity with these causes and recognize similar injustices in Mexico.[67] This overt political involvement was

63. Villafane, *Liberating Spirit*, 167–68.
64. Mier, *Las Comunidades Eclesiales de Base*, 16.
65. Aragón and Loschcke, *Iglesia de los Pobres en Nicaragua*, 27.
66. Campos, "Don Sergio Méndez Arceo," in *Don Sergio Méndez Arceo*, 117–18.
67. Ibid., 128.

met with a campaign, initiated within the United States, to discredit the CEBs and liberation theology as a religious front for communism.[68] As a result of this campaign and the intra-ecclesial confrontation with the Roman Catholic hierarchy, the involvement of the CEBs in politics has become less overt in recent years.[69] An indication of this trend was found in the more spiritual and pastoral emphasis for the Mexican national *Encuentro* of the CEBs in 1992.[70] Nevertheless the actual historical involvement of the CEBs in political issues is more demonstrable than that of the Pentecostal movement.

Microsocial Change

Challenging the commonly held view that public politics is the only way to bring about social change, Cecilia Mariz has observed how a spiritual and pastoral focus can lead to social transformation. Research on the lives of potential converts has revealed that many people are experiencing personal problems when they first attend a Pentecostal congregation. After their conversion some experience transformation of these personal problems that touch the families and community members around them.[71] Mariz places this transformation at the microsocial level. Although not overtly political, Pentecostalism enables the poor to cope with poverty and acquire skills that contribute to social and cultural change among the marginalized classes.[72]

Supporting this change at the microsocial level, Pentecostal theologian Douglas Peterson highlights several Pentecostal social service projects in Latin America which implement a self-help philosophy. In his book, *Not by Might nor by Power: A Pentecostal Theology of Social Concern in Latin America*, Peterson demonstrates that many Pentecostal groups have become involved in social service in their communities. Appropriating Martin, Peterson reasserts that rather than being

---

68. Committee of Santa Fe, "Santa Fe II," 20.

69. Dodson, "Pentecostals, Politics, and Public Space in Latin America," in Cleary and Stewart-Gambino, *Power, Politics, and Pentecostals in Latin America*, 29.

70. Otero, Fernández, and Guzmán, "Investigación de Autodiagnóstico," 74–75.

71. Bowen, *Evangelism and Apostasy*, 91.

72. Mariz, "El Pentecostalismo y El Enfrentamiento a la Pobreza en Brazil," in B. F. Gutiérrez, *En la Fuerza del Espíritu*, 204.

a movement *for* the poor, Pentecostalism is a movement *of* the poor.[73] The poor break out of cycles of dependency and help themselves resulting in empowerment and ultimately the democratization of society. Although Pentecostalism began with an emphasis on evangelism, its concern for the whole person, including physical and material needs, has gradually moved it toward a deepening social awareness.[74] He goes on to highlight specific social service projects among the poor in Latin America and an accompanying philosophy of social transformation at the micro level.

In addition to microsocial change, some Pentecostals are participating more in traditional politics. Although many Pentecostal denominations still discourage involvement in "worldly affairs," there have been several instances of Pentecostals running for political office and entire denominations voting *en bloc* for one candidate.[75] Protestant missiologist Rene Padilla observes this tendency: "Although abstention from politics still persists in evangelical circles, it is quite clear that it is now being replaced by a social engagement that could not have been imagined just a few years ago."[76]

While it is generally agreed that Pentecostals are participating more in politics, as a whole they do not represent a consistent political platform. Their beliefs have ran the gamut from a progressive city council official of the Brazilian *Partido dos Trabalhadores*[77] to the right-wing platform of Rios Montt in Guatemala in 1982. Scholarly analysis of Pentecostal participation in traditional politics ranges from Martin, in the heritage of Willems, who sees the potential for Pentecostals to transfer their symbolic protest of society to the political sphere, and others like Bastian, in the tradition of Lalive D'Epinay, who sees an authoritarian leadership style that promotes mechanisms of domination—blocking the progress of democratization.[78]

---

73. Peterson, *Not by Might, Nor by Power*, 147. Also see Martin, *Tongues of Fire*, 108.

74. Ibid., 148.

75. Bastian, *Protestantismos y Modernidad Latinoamericana*, 271.

76. Padilla, "New Actors on the Political Scene in Latin America," in Cook, *New Face of the*, 83.

77. Cox, *Fire From Heaven*, 164.

78. Bastian, *Protestantismos y Modernidad Latinoamericana*, 278.

While Pentecostal participation in the public arena is splintered, Pentecostalism's role in the private sphere has a latent effect upon the public arena. One identifiable social issue that both the CEBs and Pentecostalism have begun to impact is gender roles. In spite of the conservative theology of some Pentecostal denominations that prohibit women from preaching, the emphasis on the family and domestic responsibilities inevitably raises the status of women. In a society where common male practices of drinking, smoking and extramarital sex are considered within the norm, the Pentecostal movement has become a "strategic" woman's movement.[79] Within Protestant circles, the tendency is for women to convert first and then to evangelize along kinship lines. The "conversion" of husbands is particularly gratifying because men become subject to the same ethical standards as the wives, and thus can be held accountable for their responsibilities in the home. Elizabeth Brusco states:

> Unlike Western feminism, it is not attempting to gain access for women to the male world; rather, it elevates domesticity, for both men and women, from the devalued position it occupies as the result of the process of proletarianization. It does serve to transform gender roles, primarily by reattaching males to the family.[80]

Although woman's emancipation may not be a manifest goal of Pentecostalism, the latent effect upon Latin American society has been lifting the value of domesticity and greater gender equality.

Although the early literature of the CEBs emphasized greater awareness of economic or class inequality, the CEB's discourse on woman's liberation has gradually become more intentional.[81] Since many of the poor in Latin America are women and children, the CEBs have recently developed an intentional discourse that critiques economic oppression in relation to sexism. Parallel to this development has been increasing participation of women in leadership roles—leading to greater tension with the Roman Catholic hierarchy.[82] Many women

---

79. Busco, *Reformation of Machismo*, 6. Also see Bowen, *Evangelism and Apostasy*, 91.

80. Ibid., 3.

81. Boff, *Ecclesiogenesis*, 35.

82. Otero, Fernández, and Guzmán, "Investigación de Autodiagnóstico," 79.

have become frustrated with this "glass ceiling" within the church, and have taken their leadership skills outside the church to advance grass-root causes in secular non-governmental agencies. Therefore the CEBs have not had the direct access to re-educate men and whole families in the community. Nevertheless, the equal participation and leadership of women is emphasized in the activities and curriculum of the CEBs.

Summary

Like the impact upon gender roles, both Ecclesial Base Communities and Pentecostalism are having many manifest and latent effects in the private and public sphere in Latin America. Both movements are working among the poor with somewhat different constituencies. The members of the CEBs are not homogenous—as they have middle-class pastoral agents among them. The Pentecostals, on the other hand, often represent a more marginal sector of the population, but there are middle and upper-class congregations which do not mix with the poor. Conversion is important for the CEBs and Pentecostals, although with different interpretations of its meaning. For the CEBs, conversion is turning away from a selfish materialistic lifestyle to join the struggle for liberation in solidarity with the poor against the powers of evil. Pentecostal conversion involves a rejection of the corrupt current world order to embrace an egalitarian vision of the Reign of God.

Both the CEBs and Pentecostals carry out evangelism and discipleship in the small group setting. Reading and discussing the Bible at these gatherings result in reading and analytical skills. While conscientization is the objective of the CEBs, Bridges Johns highlights the communal memory of resistance in Pentecostalism and exhorts Pentecostals to realize their potentional of symbolic protest and engage in conscientization of social inequalities. Although the two movements have different values and content, according to Mariz, both groups equip the participant with skills to cope with, and possibly overcome poverty. Conscientization has resulted in more direct political participation for the CEBs; although recently their emphasis is more pastoral and spiritual. The Pentecostal focus on the private sphere has resulted in microsocial change, which is leading to more Pentecostal-sponsored social services in Latin America. Overall, I have found that the manifest and latent effects of the CEBs and Pentecostals among the Latin American poor have contributed toward the democratization and modernization of society. While this research is certainly open to surprises, the above review of background literature has raised these themes as important for investigation at the practical level. The ethnographic chapters to follow will attempt to "test" or at least apply these theories to specific case studies in Mexico.

Ethnographic Findings

Introduction to Part Two
Ethnographic Research

Introduction

PART TWO OF THIS STUDY WILL GROUND THE THEORETICAL UNDER-standing of Ecclesial Base Communities and Pentecostalism found in Part One with an ethnographic study of both movements. Although one cannot expect to make universal claims from the experience of one study, it is essential to apply the theoretical to the concrete. This ethnography will add accountability to the theoretical claims about both movements. As the ethnography is conducted in one specific social location, there may be points of divergence as well as convergence between the general and the particular.

In order to eliminate variables in my research methodology, I selected an Ecclesial Base Community and a Pentecostal Church in the same working-class neighborhood in Cuernavaca. Before deciding upon Colonia Alta Vista Alegre, I visited faith communities in two other *barrios*. Since there are Pentecostal churches in nearly every neighborhood in Cuernavaca, and CEBs only exist in certain *colonias*, my initial criteria forced me to find a functioning CEB local unit first, and then seek a nearby Pentecostal church. I learned of Colonia Alta Vista Alegre when a friend, who has extensive contacts among the Ecclesial Base Communities, said that she used to live in this community and offered me the telephone number of one of its leaders. I called and introduced myself as a mutual friend, and asked if it would be possible to attend a meeting of their local unit. As I drove up the main street to the CEB, I passed two large Pentecostal churches and later asked the times of their activities. I decided on the "Discípulos de Jesus" Pentecostal Church by virtue of its proximity to the Catholic church. Subsequently I asked for permission from the leaders of both organizations to carry out my research and participate in their faith communities for one year.

My rationale in selecting this particular *barrio* was that it contained both an Ecclesial Base Community and a Pentecostal church within a half-block of each other. The proximity of one to the other was helpful in minimizing the margin of error. The quality of life indicators (i.e., living conditions, employment opportunities, income, birth rate, infant mortality rate and life expectancy) would theoretically remain constant for the surrounding community which represents the pool of potential new members for both groups.

Colonia Vista Alegre started forty years ago at the southern end (closest to downtown Cuernavaca) and the newer arrivals continued to build up the mountain to the north. Although the neighborhood is generally working-class, it is not completely homogeneous. In the forty years since the neighborhood was established, some people have improved their financial lot more than others. Some have left for the United States and have sent back cash remittances to build nice homes and start businesses. At the southern end of the neighborhood the inhabitants have been established for some time and some second generation residents have gone to the university and become professionals. As a result, the economic solvency of the population is greater at the southern end than the northern. Meanwhile the newcomers are forced to build their homes further up the mountain or down into the ravines.

Description of Cuernavaca

The ethnographic study of both the Base Ecclesial Community and the Pentecostal church is based in the Colonia Vista Alegre in Cuernavaca, a city located sixty miles south of Mexico City in the state of Morelos. At one time a small provincial capital, Cuernavaca has now absorbed much of this growth in sprawling *barrios* built by the influx of migrants, to bring the current population up to 337,966.[1] Thousands of migrants have fled the economic hardships and droughts of the southern state of Guerrero to seek greater prosperity north in Cuernavaca. Approximately 40 percent of the population of Cuernavaca have migrated from other states, 40 percent of these from Guerrero.[2] In addition, some wealthy residential neighborhoods have also been built to entice middle and

1. Otero, Fernández, and Guzmán, "Investigación de Autodiagnóstico."
2. *Anuario Estadístico*, Morelos, Instituto Nacional de Estadística, 1990.

upper-class Mexicans fleeing from the earthquake,[3] crime and smog of Mexico City. Cuernavaca has an elevation of 5,058 feet which provides a year-round spring-like climate where the temperature oscillates between 70 and 90 degrees. Cuernavaca's weather has earned it the nickname, "The City of Eternal Springtime." The rainy season runs from May to October, and the dry season from November through April. Cuernavaca is located in the northwest corner of the state and the mountain streams run through Cuernavaca down into the valley. The region enjoys an ample water supply and a mild climate which allows the agricultural production year around with the principal crops being sugar cane, rice and garden vegetables. The major industries in the state are manufacturing plants, food production, textiles and oil. A research and *maquiladora*[4] park called CIVAC exists in the southeast of Cuernavaca and houses such foreign manufacturers as BASF, Nissan and Burlington Textiles.

History of the State of Morelos

Morelos was the home of revolutionary hero Emiliano Zapata who fought against the unequal distribution of land and the industrialization of dictator Porfirio Diaz who ruled Mexico from 1876 to 1911. Before the revolution, the state of Morelos belonged to thirty-two families who owned large *haciendas*.[5] Zapata's slogan, "Land and Liberty," called for the redistribution of the large estates and freedom from the dictatorship and foreign interests.[6] The victory of the Mexican Revolution allowed for the implementation of Zapata's "Plan de Ayala," guaranteeing the peasant collective ownership of land through a community trust called *ejido*.[7] Following the end of the revolution in 1919 there continued to

3. On September 19, 1985, Mexico City suffered a massive earthquake that killed 10,000 people and left several thousand homeless.

4. This is the commonly accepted term in Spanish for assembly plants. These plants prefer to assemble their products in Mexico to take advantage of lower labor costs. After the signing of the North American Free Trade Agreement in 1992 more and more companies have moved their plants to Mexico.

5. See above, 20 n. 48.

6. Miller, *Old Villages and a New Town*, 23.

7. Ibid. The Plan de Ayala is the manifesto presented by General Emiliano Zapata on November 25, 1911, calling for an end to Porfirio Diaz' and Francisco Madero's tyranny and the expropriation of 1/3 of large plantations for landless peasants to be

be much civil strife, and most of the land reform were not implemented until Lazaro Cardenas' administration from 1934–1940. While the state of Morelos was a center of revolutionary activity and advances for the peasants, other states still benefited from the "Plan de Ayala."

These changes and minor benefits must be weighed against the tremendous destruction and loss of life during the revolution. Since then, the dreams of the revolution became institutionalized, and often corrupted under the leadership of the Institutionalized Revolutionary Party (PRI). The PRI governed the country until the 2000 election of Vicente Fox of the National Action Party (PAN), who became the first non-PRI presidential candidate to rule since the revolution. Nevertheless many people still have memories, or at least have a special place for the dreams of Zapata—particularly in the state of Morelos.

In the years since the revolution, industrialization has taken place drawing migrants from neighboring states in search of work. The population of the state has grown dramatically in recent decades from 386,000 in 1960 to 616,000 in 1970, and more than doubled by the year 2000 to over one and a half million.[8]

The Residents of Colonia Alta Vista Alegre

Specifically, the Colonia Vista Alegre is located on the northwest side of Cuernavaca and is a relatively new neighborhood that has been populated primarily with migrants from neighboring states. For example, every member of the CEB that I studied was from the town of Chichioalco, Guerrero. The priest and many members of the community are astounded by the rapid urbanization of the Colonia Vista Alegre. The lay representative of the parish, who moved to the *colonia* in 1971, remembers: "All this [pointing to the neighborhood] was open fields and there was only one road up the hill. There was one bus in and one bus out of Vista Alegre everyday. If you missed that bus then you were stuck for another day."[9]

---

called "Ejidos." *Ejido* is an agrarian community named after the traditional communal lands in Indian cultures. It replaced the hacienda as the dominant social form in rural Mexico. The new system gave the peasant and small farmer freedom from the exploitative arrangements of the old estates.

8. *Anuario Estadístico*, Morelos, Instituto Nacional de Estadística, Geografía e Informática, 2000.

9. Interview with Margarita, November 3, 2001.

Now the neighborhood, like the rest of Cuernavaca, has become urbanized with many new migrants building their houses and starting businesses. According to the 1995 census, the neighborhood of Vista Alegre has a population of 3,895 in a total of 873 dwellings. The influx of inhabitants has been so fast that the city of Cuernavaca has not been able to provide adequate infrastructure, leaving 180 homes in the *colonia* without sewage disposal and another 304 without running water in the neighborhood.[10] All but sixteen homes in the neighborhood have managed to hook up electrical lines either legally or illegally. Usually plots of land are acquired and houses are built by individual initiative—rapidly outpacing the government development plan.

The migrants have come to Cuernavaca in search of work and have found openings predominantly in the service sector. Most men work in construction, factories, and the transportation industry. The women, who were not accustomed to work outside the home before arriving in Cuernavaca, often choose professions such as seamstress, domestic worker and vendor.[11] These migrants face a difficult transition to urban life and as a result undergo many sociological and psychological changes in addition to the material challenges of getting settled.

Ethnographic Methodology

Before explaining my ethnographic methodology, I would like to share my social location and theoretical perspective. In all ethnographic studies there are barriers such as language and culture, however the risk of distortion through the power dynamic involved with a North American ethnographer doing research in Latin America is even greater. Therefore I undertake the task of carrying out an ethnographic study of a Base Christian Community and a Pentecostal Church in Mexico with great trepidation. Given the postmodern critiques of anthropology I am not naive as to the power of rhetoric, nor the neo-colonial dynamics involved in this research. The complicit and implicit role of ethnographers in colonization has been well documented.[12] Therefore I must acknowledge my social location as a white, middle-class male from the

10. *Anuario Estadístico*, Morelos, Instituto Nacional de Estadística, 1995.
11. Interview with Margarita, November 3, 2001.
12. Comaroff and Comaroff, *Revelation and Revolution*, 15.

United States. At the same time I acknowledge my theoretical model to be liberationist. As it relates to the church, this means that I affirm ecclesial models that engage and empower the poor to struggle against oppression. I am also critical of church models that do not engage the poor, or are uncritical of oppressive structures. With this cultural baggage and theoretical model, fully aware that it is not possible to offer a "true" account of a culture, I cautiously begin the task of reporting my findings of a one-year ethnography of an Ecclesial Base Community and a Pentecostal Church.

In carrying out this ethnographic study, I used the participant-observer methodology, actively participating in the lives of these communities over the course of one year to attempt to gain the trust of the communities as an "insider" while observing and taking notes. Although not living in the *barrio*, I tried to be present at funerals, birthday parties, and other community events. Nevertheless, I realize that a year of field-work is a relatively short period of time and I can never fully become an "insider." In addition, I conducted interviews with informants, gathered life histories, took field notes, and recorded sermons and Bible studies. Due to space limitations, I have selected the stories of two representatives of each movement to report here. In all four cases they were leaders of their respective movements who may reflect a more apologetic attitude toward their organization. Nevertheless, their testimonies are typical and representative of the collective experience.

In order to respect the confidentiality of my informants I have assigned them pseudonyms and have changed the name of the neighborhood and the faith communities. In an effort to avoid the error of assuming that "natives" do not have agency to interpret their own culture, I have examined many sources (songs, sermons, tracks and lesson plans) that have been produced locally.[13] In the case of songs, I have passed on this content unmediated to the reader, however most material has been filtered through my lens as participant and writer. Thus I acknowledge the power of the ethnographer and writer to color one's interpretations.[14]

---

13. For further reading on the agency of the "native" to interpret their own culture, see Rosaldo, *Culture and Truth*, 50.

14. For more discussion on the power of the ethnographer as writer, see Clifford, *Predicament of Culture*, 13.

In addition to my field notes of congregational activities, I have recorded my thoughts, feelings and reactions to the events. While recording feelings would have been taboo for classical and modern schools of anthropology, I believe that my personal reactions could not be avoided as I entered into spontaneous social situations. As my personal responses became part of my field research and the way I have mediated this to the reader, hence I candidly acknowledge my feelings.[15] Although this is very subjective, at least I am transparent, and perhaps my emotions can be insightful for the reader who is unable to be there.

Since my fieldwork is carried out in Spanish, I have paid careful attention to the methodological issue of translation. In the case of key words or phrases I have maintained important terms in the original Spanish and have interpreted their meaning for the reader. For instance, terms such as *animadora, el patrón* and *barrio* remain in their Spanish form. I feel that translating specific terms into its English "equivalents" changes their original intention. For example, *Cassell's Spanish-English, English-Spanish Dictionary* translates the term *barrio* as "district" or "quarter."[16] The use of this term immediately conjures up an association with the Western, strictly geographical connotation of a district or quarter, while the Spanish connotation of *barrio* as a poor, working-class neighborhood or community is lost. This nuance and context is not communicated through the English translation. It must also be noted that all translations, by definition, are inaccurate because they take the word out of context. As a result, translation is one aspect of ethnography which offers great power to the anthropologist. Therefore, I leave most key words in their original language and I rely on my informers to define the term in their own context. This is a method appropriated from the Geertzian symbolic school of anthropology which moves from "thin" to "thick" ethnography by interpreting meaning from "the native's point of view."[17] Therefore, upon the word's first citation, I offer a definition of the term in English for the benefit of the non-Spanish speaking reader, and then contextualize it so that the reader may get a feel for the environment in which it is commonly used.

15. This method in ethnographic field work has become popular among postmodern anthropologists as a reaction against the claims of objectivity of classic ethnographers.

16. Gooch and de Paredes, *Cassell's Spanish-English, English-Spanish Dictionary*, 93.

17. Geertz, *Interpretation of Culture*, 11.

In addition to these qualitative techniques, my methodology also includes some quantitative research. Specifically, I report the statistics about the population trends in Cuernavaca in general and Vista Alegre in particular. I also carry out a survey of both faith communities. In the local unit of the CEB, without advance notice I distributed a questionnaire at one meeting where sixteen of the seventeen members (94 percent) were present. Likewise, I surveyed the Pentecostal membership at separate meetings of men and women. The total members responding to the questionnaire were forty (twenty men and twenty women) who represented 10 percent of the total four hundred baptized members of the congregation.

5

Ethnographic Findings of Field Work in an Ecclesial Base Community in Cuernavaca

Introduction

When I approached two barrels in the road serving as a barrier, I had no alternative but to park my car and walk to the end of the street. I walked up to the barrels and looked down the steep slope that the Mexicans called *la barranca*.[1] This *barrio* was built on both sides of a path looking down the ravine. As I began to negotiate my way down the steps, I could not help imagining how each brick, each sack of cement, and eventually, each refrigerator, were carried down these steps to build and furnish people's homes. I continued down the hill and asked for the address where the Ecclesial Base Communities were meeting, the home of the "La Señora Margarita," and they guided me right to her front door. Margarita was considered to be the leader of the CEBs in the Colonia de Vista Alegre. She was elected to be the representative of the parish, one of two diocesan lay leaders, and was active in many CEB training events. In this chapter, I will share the story of Margarita as part of my ethnographic findings of the Ecclesial Base Communities in the Colonia de Vista Alegre.

Background of the *Comunidades Eclesiales de Base* in Colonia de Vista Alegre

Margarita was one of several new members of the CEBs in the Colonia de Altavista in the early 1980s. But it was not always that way. After

1. The English definition of this word is ravine, but the residents attach a territorial meaning which defines their surroundings as members on the community.

a nucleus of homes was built in the *barrio*, the Roman Catholic chapel in Vista Alegre was erected in the 1970s as a mission of the San Anton parish. It finally became a parish of its own in October of 1992 when the rectory was completed and Father Marcelo Dominguez was named the parish priest of a church that I will call "Nuestra Señora de Guadalupe."

The Ecclesial Base Community existed in Colonia Alta Vista Alegre even before it officially became a parish. Since the first CEB in Cuernavaca began in Colonia Carolina in 1975 and then in San Anton, the CEBs spread throughout the city in several working-class neighborhoods before one was established in Vista Alegre in 1982. But even before Vista Alegre had fully organized CEBs, the priest in San Anton, Jose Luis Calvillo, planted the seeds by starting Bible study groups (although these were not yet considered Base Communities because they did not use the same methodology).[2] Margarita was one of the early leaders in the *colonia* to learn about the CEBs and fall in love with their methodology.

The Life Story of Margarita

Margarita and her husband, Manuel, had arrived in Cuernavaca in 1971. In spite of their leadership as catechists in their home parish in Guerrero, they did not immediately get involved in church work in Cuernavaca. They were too preoccupied with the daily tasks of survival and adjustment to the new urban environment. Manuel found a job as a handyman with the municipal government and Margarita was a homemaker and sold some merchandise on the side to make ends meet. Margarita admitted that they were primarily concerned with their own well-being and were not interested in the world around them. In 1980, Juliana Santos, an elderly woman who was active in the parish, invited them to a pilgrimage for *La Virgin de Guadalupe*. They participated in the procession and then Margarita accepted an invitation to participate in a Bible reflection group. While she enjoyed studying the Bible, the group was not yet considered a CEB until a new priest came with a different methodology.

2. Although Bible studies were held previously in the parish, the beginning of the CEBs is marked by their unique methodology. For more on the method, see chapter 3.

Father Rogelio Orozco was assigned to the San Anton parish in 1982 and traveled to Vista Alegre to teach the CEB methodology to the previously-formed Bible study reflection groups. He brought the *to see*, to *judge*, and *to act* method that later was expanded to include two further steps: *to evaluate* and *to celebrate*.[3] This method encouraged a critical reflection on the unjust living conditions. Margarita explains her experience with this new methodology:

> I like the method because it allows one to analyze reality in light of the Bible and then to act to change reality. Sometimes when we don't have any curriculum for our study, we just ask what happened that week. We would begin a whole lesson just analyzing the current events in light of the Bible.[4]

The arrival of Father Orozco, the training of lay people, and the introduction of the new praxis method of Bible study marked the emergence of the CEBs in Vista Alegre.

In 1982 Bishop Méndez Arceo was forced to retire from the episcopacy, yet the CEB network in Cuernavaca remained strong, and was even expanding. Young leaders like Margarita, then thirty-four years of age, were barely getting started with new communities like the Colonia de Vista Alegre. Margarita speaks both for herself and for her husband as she shares the impact of participating in the CEBs:

> We were transformed completely. Before participating in the CEBs we were completely apathetic and distant from the church . . . Since arriving in Cuernavaca we had lived completely oblivious to the world around us. But when we got involved [with the CEBs] I became interested. Before I was only preoccupied with my own business, but afterwards I was concerned about the world around us. I started being a subject instead of an object.[5]

In spite of Bishop Méndez Arceo's departure from the diocese, the CEBs continued to grow during the 1980s.[6] This was true not only throughout Mexico, but also in other countries such as Nicaragua, Brazil, and Peru. But difficult times lay ahead as the Roman Catholic Church gradually replaced or re-located the bishops and priests who

---

3. Grupos de Estudio y Reflexión, *Comunidades Eclesiales de Base*, 24.

4. Interview with Margarita, November 3, 2001.

5. Ibid.

6. Leñero, Fernández, and Guzmán, "Investigación de Autodiagnóstico."

had encouraged CEBs. The CEBs entered a time of crisis and stagnation in the 1990s.[7]

While the Roman Catholic Church was experiencing internal struggle, the marginal *barrios* continued to grow. In Vista Alegre, for example, new arrivals were forced to build their shacks further off the main road on steep slopes. They scrambled to piece together a shelter with tin, pieces of plastic and scrap lumber. Those who had arrived sooner were able to settle in and build more permanent structures. The *colonia* as a whole developed greatly as the main streets were paved, businesses were started and schools were built. In spite of the growth of the *colonia*, the membership and leadership of the CEBs remained stagnant. By 1990 the original members of the CEBs were aging and the CEBs entered a time of crisis. In October of 1992, Vista Alegre finally became its own parish and this transition brought the assignment of a new priest. But what would the relationship be between the para-church structure of the CEBs and the official Roman Catholic parish?

Ecclesial Church Structure

As a renewal movement within the Roman Catholic Church, the CEBs have an awkward relationship with the institutional church.[8] The CEBs do not intend to separate from or replace the existing structure; on the contrary they benefit from the universal infrastructure of the Roman Catholic Church.[9] In fact the CEBs hope to co-exist with the institutional church and infuse it with a communitarian grass-roots spirit. Yet on a practical level, the antagonism of the hierarchy has caused the CEBs to set up a parallel structure to support and unite the individual local units. The CEBs call this support network "articulation," which is the connection between local units nationally within Mexico and abroad. It is the means of organization, communication and support that enables local units to feel part of a larger network. In some parishes the priest is collaborative and there are several CEBs within the ecclesial structure that support each other. Other local units of the CEBs

7. Interview with Socorro Martinez, December 5, 2001.

8. This renewal movement is to be distinguished from the Catholic Charismatic Renewal (CCR) which began with events at Duquesne University and Notre Dame University in 1967. For more information see Burgess and McGee, *Dictionary of Pentecostal and Charismatic Movements*, 135.

9. Boff, *Ecclesiogenesis*, 7.

are isolated and face opposition from the parish priest.[10] To facilitate this support network, the CEBs in Mexico have established a structure which is headed by a nationally elected team of representatives made up of four lay people from the grass roots and four religious. This *Equipo Nacional* (National Team) provides volunteer leadership and decides on the direction of the movement. They function as an executive committee and oversee the work of a small group of paid staff who work at the CEBs' national offices in Mexico City. The staff is made up of an executive secretary, two assistants, some volunteers and interns. This national office carries out the national agenda by producing resources, facilitating retreats and coordinating efforts among the nation-wide network of local communities.

CEBs are organized in 50 of the 90 Roman Catholic dioceses located in twelve regions throughout the country. In Cuernavaca, which has historically been a CEB stronghold, there is a CEB office housed in the cathedral. In the days of Bishop Méndez Arceo this office received financial support from the diocese. Today there is no full-time staff and the space is only used for the monthly planning of the *sub-districto* and other occasional meetings. Within other dioceses there are several parishes that may or may not have CEBs. For example, in the Nuestra Señora de Guadalupe parish there were 17 local units, compared to other parishes with one or two. Since the official structure of the Roman Catholic Church is no longer supportive of the CEBs, "articulation" is crucial to facilitating communication between local units in different parishes, dioceses, sub-districts and regions.

Following the meeting of CELAM II in Puebla in 1979, a conservative backlash began against the CEBs within the Roman Catholic Church.[11] Within certain dioceses and parishes the bishop or priest was overtly antagonistic to the presence of CEBs.[12] For instance, following the retirement of Bishop Sergio Méndez Arceo, the CEBs in Cuernavaca underwent a time of crisis. Previously they had received the support of the bishop and benefited from the church's infrastructure. Afterwards, the CEBs were forced to be autonomous and rely on their own resources. Something very similar has happened on a national level. In spite

10. Interview with Socorro Martinez, December 5, 2001.
11. Mier, *Las Comunidades Eclesiales de Base*, 134.
12. Interview with Socorro Martinez, December 5, 2001.

of the opposition from the hierarchy, the *Equipo Nacional* oversees a nationwide network that has an *encuentro* every four years, yearly regional retreats, monthly diocesan meetings, and weekly parish training meetings for the *animadores,* all of which connect back to local CEBs.

In the Nuestra Señora de Guadalupe parish where I did my field work, the priest gave lip service to the CEBs, but devoted most of his time and energy to the traditional sacramental activities of the parish: baptisms, weddings and catechism for first communions. Nevertheless, in an interview Father Bernardo acknowledged the strength of the CEBs in the parish. He called the CEBs the "backbone"[13] of the parish because they supplied the volunteers for the "*Pobres Serviendo Pobres*" (Poor serving the Poor) meal for children, the clinic and catechism. Nevertheless he did not help with the CEBs weekly training session for *animadores* and only occasionally attended the workshops. Most CEB members attended mass at least once a month and some attended very regularly. Thus, one might say that in the Nuestra Señora de Guadalupe parish the CEBs functioned as a "para-church" structure. The seventeen local units of the CEBs operated independently of the official parish structure, yet complemented the official church activities.

Composition of the Membership

All of the members of the Ecclesial Base Community in this parish come from the same home town of Chichioalco, Guerrero. They are mostly women who had moved to Cuernavaca in their early twenties in search of employment, and now are between the ages of forty and sixty and are mothers and grandmothers. On the average the women have a third grade education. Six of the sixteen surveyed in the CEB had completed primary school, four are illiterate and the rest have some primary. The women encourage their children and grandchildren to get an education and are willing to make sacrifices for them to study. Due to the cost of raising children, paying tuition, books and transportation to and from school, a family must prioritize and select the most promising children for advanced studies. Although the family may earn a decent income, advanced studies are quite expensive in Mexico. A majority of the women are homemakers or work part-time two or three days a week. Those who work are employed as domestic servants,

13. Interview with Father Bernardo, November 30, 2001.

vendors and seamstresses. The husbands work full-time as taxi-drivers, masons, plumbers, and waiters, and four have left for better pay in the United States. Some previously worked in the United States and have returned with some capital to start a business or finish building their home. Almost all the women have immediate family in the United States—husbands, sons, daughters, brothers, and sisters.

The members arrived from Chichioalco without any money and have begun a new life in the city. In some cases they obtained property by "squatting" on an unoccupied plot of land on the hillside or renting a house until they could purchase a plot. However all the members had a difficult time getting started and built their homes from scratch—one bag of cement at a time. Now, 20 or 30 years later, all the members have sturdy and relatively comfortable concrete homes. The houses are not luxurious, but usually have two stories, two or three bedrooms, kitchen, dining room, living room, electricity, indoor plumbing and the basic household appliances (refrigerator, stove, microwave, blender, and sometimes a washing machine). In some cases the homes are still "under construction" or "in process" as they continue to improve their home as resources become available. When asked if they were better or worse off now than ten years ago, 80 percent of the women responded that they were better off now. The stability of being in one place and having steady employment, and perhaps the remittances of a family member sending money from the United States, has allowed them to improve their quality of life.

According to a survey conducted in the CEB, the members consider themselves poor and identify with the interests of the working-class, yet the income of the members varies greatly. In some cases the adult children have married and continue to live at home—adding a second or third income to the family. Others have adult children and relatives in the United States make monthly contributions to the family economy. These sources of income, coupled with the husband's low-paying but stable employment, provide a steady income allowing the women time to participate in the CEBs. The average family income in CEBs ranges from $4,000 to $15,000 Mexican pesos a month (U.S. $400 to $1500).[14] The higher end represents families with two or three working adults, while the lower end reflects the women living without the

14. Questionnaire conducted among the CEB members.

financial support of a husband or adult child. Although the members of the local unit I studied are not wealthy, clearly their family has achieved some economic stability and the women have the "luxury" of not working full-time and volunteering for the CEB.

The CEB membership is comprised entirely of women, although an occasional husband will participate out of a sense of obligation when he and his wife are hosting the meeting in their home. When men were invited to participate on two occasions, they politely declined, joking that their wives would pray for them. Although the men do not show a great interest in attending, they do believe in God and generally support their wives' participation. When two men said that their work schedule prevented them from participating in the Friday afternoon meetings, the women stated that they would be willing to change the meeting time to accommodate their husbands but the women never followed through on this offer. The participants recalled that a man had attended regularly for several months before dropping out, apparently due to the awkwardness of being the only man. This may be an indication that the content of an all-women's Bible reflection group develops an ethos of healing and support for women in which a man does not feel welcome or it may suggest that the women in the group prefer an all-women's group creating a safe space to share without the intrusion of a man. The 5:00 pm starting time hinders the participation of working persons, both men and women, who are not able to get home from work this soon.

Women have often asked for prayers for their husbands and several report dissatisfaction in their marriages, but do not share intimate details. I was the only man attending the majority of meetings, and in spite of feeling welcome, it is likely that my presence inhibited the women's ability to share openly about gender issues. Five of the women in the group are not currently living with their husbands, due to separation, divorce or immigration to the United States. All the married women try to have the chores done and dinner prepared before they go to the meeting. Although the husbands do not attend, the women appear to be thankful that they are allowed to participate—unlike cases of *machismo*[15] where the husband prohibits the

15. The closest English term for *machismo* is male chauvinism, although in Mexican culture this is not only a personal attitude, but a systemic male privilege present throughout society.

wife's attendance. I did notice, however, that there were two women in particular who become nervous about how their husbands might react when the meetings run late.

The CEB Activities

The meetings are scheduled to begin Fridays at 5:00 p.m., but generally do not start until 5:15 or 5:20. All the members live within walking distance—most within a couple of blocks. The meeting begins when the *animadora* calls the group to order and invites the group to sing one or two songs while the stragglers arrive. On the average, the meeting has 11 people in attendance, although 17 women are considered to be regular members. Once the majority have arrived, the *animadora* begins the lesson, which is based on guidance received in a preparatory training meeting held in the parish church the previous Tuesday. She asks a volunteer or two to read the Bible passage out loud. Most of the women bring their Bibles, although there are four women in the group who are illiterate. For their sake, the *animadora* often requests a second volunteer to repeat the Bible reading.

After the leader gives a brief introduction of the lesson, she asks open-ended questions about what was learned from the passage. Oftentimes the group is timid or fearful of giving the wrong answer, so responses come forth sparingly. Then the *animadora* asks more direct questions to focus the group on her intended subject matter. About thirty to forty minutes of questions and dialogue then follow. The Bible passage and its implications for the Mexican context are analyzed. Sometimes the interpretation is related to the larger international context, such as the September 11 terrorist attacks on the twin towers and the ensuing war on terrorism. The interpretation may also take on a local flavor in relation to a recent occurrence in the neighborhood.

After this discussion and dialogue, the *animadora* concludes and tries to integrate the discussion into a brief liturgy. Usually this closing worship is part of the lesson plan and is congruent with the theme for that day. Then the group stands and concludes with an open community prayer, inviting all to participate by voicing a concern or a prayer of thanksgiving with the group responding: "Lord, listen to our prayer," or "We give you thanks O God." Then the group recites the Hail Mary or the Lord's Prayer in unison. Like all good Catholics who have been through Catechism, the members have these prayers memorized and the leader simply begins the prayer and the rest join in.

After this closing liturgy, everyone sits down while the *animadora* announces the upcoming activities and events, such as workshops, fundraisers and processions in the parish. There are often decisions to be made, money to be collected, or matters to be clarified. The group seems to enjoy this time at the end of the meeting unless it runs late. Meanwhile, refreshments are served and there is time for informal sharing and gossip. The refreshments usually consist of cookies and juice, but one Friday a month the hostess will serve *pozole*.[16] Since the content of the meeting is so structured and intellectual, the informal fellowship at the end allows a space that helps to build community. Nevertheless, it was surprising that even though the group was all women, more intimate concerns about family problems were not shared. This may take place in other more informal settings that I was unaware of, but certainly the formal lesson focused more on social justice than personal issues. The meeting normally finishes around 7:00 PM with a few women rushing home immediately and others staying for fellowship.

Generally the Ecclesial Base Communities are supportive of popular Mexican religious traditions. Margarita entered the CEBs through an invitation to participate in a pilgrimage in honor of *La Virgin de Guadalupe*, and pointed out that this continues to be an opportunity for evangelism of the populace. Thus, the CEBs honor popular religious beliefs by incorporating religious festivals and customs into their calendar of events. In Mexico each small town has a patron saint who has a day assigned to him. The town will honor this saint with festivities such as a town fair, rodeo and parade. When residents migrate to the cities they often take these religious and cultural customs with them.

The CEBs have adapted this grass-roots religious custom into their commemoration of *los excluidos* (the excluded). On the October 12 anniversary of Christopher Columbus' arrival on American soil, the CEBs have a pilgrimage to commemorate the *Dia de la Raza*.[17] The partici-

---

16. *Pozole* is a typical Mexican dish that is corn soup with chicken strips, onions, chile, and oregano. The CEBs try to encourage local traditions over and against foreign foods and customs.

17. *Dia de la Raza* ("Day of the Race" in English) a day observed throughout Mexico to mark Christopher Columbus's arrival in the Americas. It is the Mexican equivalent of Columbus Day in the United States. The CEBs' pilgrimage is unusual only in that it remembers society's outcasts.

pants carry the statue of *La Virgin de Guadalupe* and have readings to recall the injustice perpetrated against the indigenous. The exploited, the unemployed and marginalized are also remembered in the readings.

Later that same month Margarita announced a pilgrimage that would be held in the community on three consecutive days in honor of the "triune God." Each day the members would go down a different path in the neighborhood and stop at five stations representing the five mysteries of the cross. When I arrived the leaders were decorating each station with a tablecloth, candles, and an icon of the Virgin. The pilgrimage was scheduled to begin at 5:00 p.m. and the members of three local CEB units: "Jesus, Agua de Vida," "Nuevo Amanecer," and "Jésus y sus Discípulos," were invited to participate. Gradually the people assembled and Margarita called the group of about twenty together with a song. A plastic bag of beans was passed around and we were all invited to take a handful to be planted at the last station. After we began, others in the community joined the pilgrimage along the way as they returned from work or saw us passing their houses. The Protestant families chose not to participate and stayed inside their houses. Five families who were members of the CEBs and lived along the path were asked to set up the stations and to receive the pilgrimage on their porches. At each station a different lay person was in charge of leading the *novenario*. The *novenario*, from the Spanish *nueve*, is a repetition of the Hail Mary or the Prayer of Jesus nine times—one prayer for each bead on the rosary. As the leader ran her fingers down the rosary, she would begin each prayer, and the group would follow in unison. After nine prayers and a song, the procession would continue to the next station of the cross.

Two hours later the pilgrimage, having grown to thirty-seven participants, reached the final station at the end of a narrow, rugged and steep path overlooking the ravine. After completing the rosary a bucket full of dirt was passed around and all were invited to plant the beans as a symbol of the death of Jesus Christ that gives birth to new life. As an offering to God and one another, the participants opened their bags and purses and shared refreshments such as cookies, oranges, *jicama*,[18] juice, and Coca-Cola. Nearing sunset, the procession was concluded with announcements about upcoming activities and the group returned down the path to their homes.

18. *Jicama* is a juicy root that is native to Morelos and is often placed in *Piñatas* along with oranges and candy.

The Teachings of the CEBs

The curriculum for all CEB meetings is developed in the *sub-districto* by Father Marcelo Dominguez at the CEB's coordinating office in the Cathedral of Cuernavaca. The parish representative, Margarita, attends a monthly meeting of the *sub-districto* and receives the curriculum for the month. She then returns to the parish where the *animadores* are trained in the weekly Tuesday night meetings. The curriculum is written by priests and lay people and published by grass-roots organizations such as the *Secretaria Ejecutiva* of the CEBs in Mexico City, DABAR publishing house, and *Mision por la Fraternidad*.[19]

One lesson studied the passage in Acts 2:42–47 which describes life in the early church. The leader asked the community to study each verse carefully and identify the characteristics of the early church. They mentioned: teaching one another, fellowship, breaking bread, praying together, common ownership, helping the needy, generosity, and praising God together. Then the leader asked the group to analyze how we were performing as a community in comparison to the early church. They responded that they pray together and support each other, but also admitted that they need to be more generous and united as a group.

Another lesson was entitled, "In the CEBs we want to live with the dignity of children of God who reject all unjust dependency." This lesson plan came directly from the curriculum produced by DABAR publishing house in Mexico City.[20] The meeting began with two songs and a prayer before entering into the material. Then the leader asked a volunteer to read Gen 9:5–6 (an excerpt from the story of Noah where God announces a reckoning for every human being that sheds the blood of another human). The passage was read a second time for the benefit of the illiterate and those without Bibles. Then the *animadora* asked: "What are the forms of dependence through which we humans enslave and destroy each other?[21] As the community responded the leader wrote the answers on newsprint: "lack of comprehension, disobedience of commandments, lack of respect, lack of love, lack of communication, selfishness, destroying nature, resentment, apathy, ambition, indifference, ingratitude, lack of patience, laziness, pretexts, and fights." In the

19. These are all Mexican-based organizations and publishing houses.

20. The material is entitled, Mier, *Las Comunidades Eclesiales de Base*.

21. Ibid., 16.

aftermath of the September 11 terrorist attacks, the question arose as to what role Christians can play in developing a more peaceful world. The issue of the war in Afghanistan was raised, but there was a feeling that it was a very complex and distant problem of which they had little grasp or power to change from Mexico. Then again, this may have only been my interpretation of their lack of concrete suggestions.

Then the leader brought the discussion back to the concrete problems over which they did have control and asked the group: "What should we do to reject these dependencies and be faithful to the Spirit of the Gospel?"[22] To this question the community responded: "love each other, know the Word of God and transmit it to others, live and work in community, live in harmony with our family, be healthy, respect nature, support life, listen to the priests that orient us, be thankful for our daily bread, and be thankful for our Savior." Following the participation of the community, the leader elaborated on how we can reject the dependencies and slavery that destroy humans. After the Bible study the session continued with a prayer of confession inviting members to admit the ways in which they participate in dependence. This meeting concluded with an exhortation to respect the dignity of human beings.

On another occasion, the *animadora* did not start with a Bible passage, but rather asked the group to select a current event, not a sensationalized event in the media, but a local occurrence. The group volunteered three noteworthy events that had occurred that week in the *barrio*. When the leader asked the group to focus on the one event that had caused the most impact, they selected the case of a man who had fallen and opened a gash in his forehead. I was surprised that the group selected an isolated accident rather than a more transcendent issue with systemic causes. Then the leader asked the group to select a Bible passage to help us to reflect on the event. The parable of the Good Samaritan was suggested as an example of loving one's neighbor in a time of need. Again I was surprised that the group's interpretation of this passage centered on a superficial benevolent love of neighbor, rather than an analysis of the ethnicity issue involving Jews and Samaritans in the passage. So far, the group had completed the first two steps of the methodology: *to see* and *to think*.

22. Ibid.

Next the leader asked the group for a concrete action to respond to the event and suggested that a delegation from the CEB visit the injured man to express their love and concern. So three people volunteered to visit him on Sunday after mass and offer him Holy Communion.[23] This marked the third stage, *to act*. Once a concrete action was organized the *animadora* asked the group to evaluate the meeting. People offered both positive and negative feedback about the process of the meeting, but I refrained from sharing my thoughts (as stated above). Then the leader said that the only step from the methodology they had as yet not utilized was *to celebrate*, so she asked people to stand to sing a song. The meeting concluded with a song followed by announcements and refreshments. The *animadora* on this occasion was explicitly making reference to the CEB's methodology. I felt as though this was for my benefit, but I did witness several occasions when the members of the CEBs were reminded of, and even quizzed on, the stages of the method. The philosophy behind the methodology is to reflect on the praxis, or struggle, currently taking place in the lives of members.

On yet another occasion the action was local and more pastoral. A man in the neighborhood was experiencing kidney failure and was told by the doctor that only a kidney transplant could save him. The CEB found out about his illness and decided to visit him instead of having the regular meeting. We met at 5:00 and collected a spontaneous love offering among the members of the CEB. Then we selected a psalm to read as a group, had a brief business meeting and walked down the path beside the creek to his home. I asked Margarita if he was a member of their community. She replied: "He is a member of our community, but not a member of our religious community," then went on to explain that his wife used to be a member of the CEB, but had since ceased to attend. The man lived at the bottom of the ravine and I could not imagine walking along these steep slopes with kidney failure. While walking down this treacherous path beside the creek it was hard to imagine that downtown Cuernavaca was just a couple miles away. We carried out the visit, presented the offering (which came to about $30 U.S.), sang, prayed and shared a word of hope with the man. As we returned along the steep path I asked how the man was able to get to the hospital for

23. Lay people who receive training are authorized by the priest to be "ministers" and take holy communion to persons in their home; Margarita had received this training and authorization.

his check-ups, and the others responded that the neighbors in the community formed a human chain to carry him up the hill. This action of the CEBs was to be in solidarity with this man.

Hymnology

The songs sung in the Ecclesial Base Communities are from a hymnal entitled "Cantemos en Comunidad: Hacia la Justicia por el Evangelio" ("Let's Sing in Community: Toward Justice for the Gospel"). This songbook was published by the Commission of Music and Liturgy of the Diocese of Cuernavaca in 1982. The hymnal is a collection of songs sung by the Ecclesial Base Communities around Latin America and Mexico. It was compiled for the CEBs during the episcopacy of Bishop Sergio Méndez Arceo. The preface of the hymnal describes the theological content of the songs as follows:

> This songbook offers a great abundance of songs for all occasions. Therefore, its use is not exclusively for a liturgical assembly, but for all groups that meet to reflect upon their liberating march. There are not two realities, only one [person] that seeks liberation in one's religious self and in one's struggles with one's brothers and sisters.

The hymns in the songbook are organized according to themes such as justice, issues, folk songs, the Virgin Mary, the Eucharist and seasons of the liturgical calendar. The hymnal also contains the songs from the popular masses developed in Nicaragua, El Salvador, Panama and locally in Cuernavaca. The lyrics are printed with guitar chords, but without the musical notes. The songbook also contains a guide for guitar players, although most local units of the CEBs do not have musicians and must sing *acapela*.

One of the favorite songs of the local unit "Jesus, Agua de Vida," is a tribute to mother Mary. Entitled "A Ti Madre" (To You Mother), it describes Mary gives hope, love and courage in the midst of brokenness. The popularity of this song in the CEB meetings is an indicator of the centrality of the Virgin Mary in CEB theology. The lyrics are as follows:

Chorus: To you mother of hope, to you mother of love,
To you mother of men, to you I sing my song.

Verse 1: You put happiness in our lives,
You are tender and comprehensive;
You smile and wait when you call us,
Every day you are a new inspiration.

Verse 2: If everything fails in our journey,
If we forget to give God the "yes,"
You renew the courage in our lives
And make us laugh again.[24]

This song emphasizes the maternal qualities of the Virgin Mary as accompaniment along life's journey. In the midst of hardships and failure, Mary is the inspiration providing hope, life and happiness. In Mexican society in general, and particularly for a group of women, the status of motherhood is very high. In this predominantly Roman Catholic society, and especially among the CEBs, mother Mary embodies the positive qualities of hope, love and courage. Her accompaniment along the journey of brokenness offers an image of empowerment to the women of the CEBs.

The metaphor of life as a journey continues in another favorite song entitled, "Iglesia Peregrina" (Pilgrim Church). This song has been sung at several meetings and makes reference to the CEB ecclesiology. The lyrics are:

All united forming one body,
A people that Christmas gave birth to;
Members of Christ in blood redeemed,
Pilgrim church of God.
The force of the Spirit lives in us.
As the Son was sent by the Father,
He impels, guides and feeds us,
Pilgrim church of God.[25]

Following the biblical motif of the Hebrews' liberation from slavery in Egypt and journey to the promised land, the CEBs place a theological emphasis on being a pilgrim church journeying toward liberation. They consider themselves to be "the church in movement, rather than a

24. Ibid., 19; my translation.
25. Ibid., 91.

movement of the church."[26] Another name for the CEBs is the "Church of the Poor," which reflects their identity as a group seeking liberation on behalf of the poor. Although they are spread throughout Mexico, they remain united as members of the body of Christ.[27] They know that God accompanies them on this journey and that their destiny will be the fulfillment of the promise of the Reign of God.

Leadership and Empowerment

One theme that became evident from conversations with the women was a sense of self-esteem and empowerment acquired through participation in the CEBs. Through interviews and questionnaires I was able to further ascertain the impact that participation in the CEBs had on the women. Given their limited opportunities for education, initially most of the women felt uncomfortable about participating in the meetings. Nevertheless, the all-woman composition of the membership and the relaxed environment created a safe setting conducive to learning and sharing. Although the relatively short length of my field work (one year) was too limited to ascertain long-term growth, the women testified to and expressed gratitude for having learned to think and speak in public over the years of their participation. When asked what they learned the most from their participation in the CEBs, 37.5 percent answered "to serve their neighbor," and another 25 percent responded "to read the Bible."[28] Participation in the CEBs has empowered the women to have more self-esteem and more concern for others.

In spite of it being an option on the questionnaire, the members did not respond that politics was one of the areas that they had learned the most about through their participation in the CEBs. Another question in the survey was: "Should the Church be involved in politics?"[29] Only 10 percent said yes, with 70 percent responding "little." While the women seemed to show indifference to involvement in politics, it is important to recall that according to the Mexican constitution institu-

26. Interview with Margarita, November 3, 2001.

27. Reference to 1 Corinthians 12.

28. Questionnaire conducted among the CEB members.

29. Ibid.

tional church is prohibited from participation in politics.[30] In hindsight the questionnaire may have revealed more inclination toward politics had it used a different term like "social justice." Although the women had been empowered, they were not more inclined to participate in politics.

In 1992 when Father Marcelo became the new parish priest, he immediately noticed the need to cultivate potential leaders. At that time Carmen was a youth in the community who liked the church, but needed encouragement. She explains how she entered the CEBs:

> I got married in 1980 when I was 19 years-old and at first I was not involved in anything. I remember Father Jose Luis Calvillo visited the homes in the neighborhood and gave studies. I liked to listen in to what the priest said, but I was not active in the parish. Finally, in 1984, Margarita started to invite the people to a Bible reflection group. I liked it from the beginning and attended regularly. Margarita told me that I had the aptitude to be an *animadora*, but I told her that it was too much work. On a few occasions she wasn't able to attend the meeting, and asked me to go in her place. At first I was very nervous and didn't know what to do, but she told me to do the same thing she did. In retrospect, I think she made up an excuse not to attend just to give me the opportunity to lead. But I was still not a regular *animadora*. Then in 1997 we received a new priest, Father Marcelo, and he said that the CEBs must start to produce fruit. He said that the CEBs had been working for several years, and always had the same leaders. He said that I would be a good *animadora*. Then he gave the order that all the *animadores* must bring a second person from the local unit to the training events and meetings as a substitute. So this is how I started going to the meetings for *animadores*. Then in 1999 I started full time as *animadora* of my own unit.[31]

Today Carmen is the *animadora* for one of the newest local units called "Jesus, Agua de Vida" (Jesus, Water of Life). Although she is one of

30. Beginning with the administration of Porfirio Diaz in 1876 the state protected religious liberty (for both Protestants and Catholics) under the unstated condition that the church not involve itself in politics. After the adoption of the 1917 constitution, clergy were forbidden to vote, or criticize, in public or private, "the fundamental laws of the country, the authorities in particular, or the government in general." (Rabasa and Caballero, *Mexicano*, Article 130. Also see Bowen, *Evangelism and Apostasy*, 29–33 and Rosales, *Estado e Iglesia en México*.)

31. Interview with Carmen, November 2, 2001.

the youngest *animadoras*, she has earned the respect of her peers. Jesus, Agua de Vida was formed in 1999 after a missionary effort of the CEBs to reach families who were not attending. Carmen explains how this new unit of CEBs was formed:

> I accompanied Margarita on a missionary campaign in the neighborhood. We targeted a little neighborhood down the ravine from my house, because we noticed that there were many families who did not participate in a CEB. A few of us went door-to-door asking people if they would be interested in joining the CEBs. A few said yes and a few said no. We also asked them when would be the best day and time for a meeting. We kept those names and a few months later Margarita said it was time to invite them to a meeting. We asked one of the neighbors to host the meeting in her home. The first meeting was a great success: there were sixteen people between adults and children. After that Margarita asked me to be the *animadora* and so I continued meeting every week with that group. Some of the first people left, and some new people joined, but the group is still meeting.[32]

I also had the opportunity to participate in a missionary campaign during my research in the community. The first three days of Holy Week, which traditionally are holidays, were dedicated to visiting potential members. Margarita and Carmen invited the group to join them every afternoon at 4:00 to assign the visitations. Then we split up in pairs, visiting houses of the non-active persons in the neighborhood. Some people attended mass, but did not want to have the additional commitment of joining a CEB. Others expressed an interest and were invited to attend the CEB activities. Their names and addresses were noted for further reference. There were also a substantial number of families who identified themselves as evangelicals and did not want to associate with any Roman Catholic group.

It was this same type of missionary campaign that gave birth to the existing CEB. The Jesus, Agua de Vida, group started in 1999 and continues to meet every Friday night. In addition to the new people, some members of other local units have transferred in to augment the group. From the example of Carmen and the other participants in the

---

32. Ibid.; my translation.

CEB, I conclude that the empowerment of the participants of the CEBs has been on a personal, rather than on a public or political level.

Social Action and Political Involvement

The background literature produced by Latin American liberation theologians in the 1970s and 1980s heavily emphasized the social involvement of the CEBs in the struggles for liberation. As times and context have changed since the early literature about CEBs was written, I became particularly interested in obtaining information about the CEBs' current political participation through one local unit in Mexico.

As has been noted, action is built into the methodology of each lesson plan. In my observations, however, the meetings only occasionally result in an action. Once, at the conclusion of a meeting, a member expressed her concern about loose dogs in the neighborhood. Other members commented on the lack of hygiene, safety for children, and the discourtesy of owners who do not clean up after their dogs. The response of the CEB was to name a group of three women to go to the local clinic and ask for the phone number of the city office for animal control. The following week it was reported that the women acquired the phone number. I do not know if they called animal control, but the problem continued. As already stated, another meeting resulted in the naming of a delegation to visit a man who had fallen and express the love and concern of the CEB for his well-being. On another occasion the meeting of *animadores* from the Cuernavaca *sub-districto* decided to collect medicines for the indigenous population in Chiapas. The following week one person brought a donation.

At the end of another meeting the problem of trash pick-up in the neighborhood was discussed. This is quite complicated since many families live down in the ravine where the garbage truck has no access. They bring their garbage up to a designated pick-up spot on the road, but if the truck does not come they just leave their garbage—thus attracting dogs and flies. A community-based sanitation committee had called for a public meeting to discuss the issue, so the CEB agreed to support the work of this committee. These actions, in addition to the previously-mentioned visit to a man with kidney failure, were the only ones in which I participated and witnessed.

In all fairness, it is difficult to get a complete picture of the CEBs while attending one local unit for only a year. Nevertheless, based on my experience, I found only occasional action and most of it was benevolent acts of kindness with little systematic analysis. Interviews with leaders of the CEBs who had had a greater involvement beyond the local unit were helpful in learning about political participation in the past.

When Margarita first became involved with the CEBs in the early 1980s, she was very innocent about the world around her. She began to learn about solidarity with other struggles for liberation in Central America. She recalls:

> At that time there were a lot of refugees from El Salvador living in the neighborhood and the CEBs began a relationship with them. They had fled El Salvador because of oppression and persecution for their religious and political beliefs. The CEBs helped them with their basic needs and in the exchange we learned a lot. They taught us about the reality in their country and about Central America. This helped us gain a consciousness and to become interested in similar problems in our country and government. The solidarity began with Don Sergio Mendez Arceo whom I met on just a few occasions before his retirement.[33]

From the legacy of Bishop Méndez Arceo, the CEBs acquired a commitment to solidarity with the oppressed. Through these exchanges with Salvadorans CEBs acquired some tools of analysis to understand their own Mexican reality.

Another action of the CEB occurred in 1994 when some developers with ties to the government attempted to build a country club for the wealthy in the nearby town of Tepotzlán. The plans included the building of a golf course which would use up a considerable amount of the town's water supply to water the greens. The town leaders began to organize against this plan and held a strike. Blocking off the main road coming into Tepotzlán, the townsfolk did not let traffic in or out. The local CEB unit communicated the stand-off to the CEBs in Cuernavaca (about 20 miles away) and asked for support. So CEBs collected food and, in order to bypass the roadblock, took it on foot to Tepotzlán.[34] The resistance of the townsfolk, with the help of outside solidarity, succeeded in thwarting the efforts of the developers.

33. Interview with Margarita, November 3, 2001; my translation.
34. Interview with Carmen, November 2, 2001.

The leadership of the CEBs has also been in solidarity with the Zapatista movement in Chiapas. On January 1, 1994 *the Ejercito Zapatista de Liberación Nacional* (the Zapatista Army for National Liberation) began an uprising to fight for the respect and dignity of indigenous languages, cultures and lands. Leaders from the CEBs in Cuernavaca traveled on delegations to Chiapas to learn about the issues and life conditions of the indigenous people there. In addition, representatives from the indigenous communities have visited Cuernavaca to talk about their struggle and to raise funds. Local units of CEBs have sent medicine, used clothing and money to the indigenous communities.[35] Through the leadership, the CEBs in Cuernavaca have shown their solidarity with the cause of the Zapatistas in Chiapas with these concrete actions.

During national and local elections the CEBs organize a panel of candidates to inform their members as to the issues and platforms of leading parties. One particularly contentious election took place on July 5, 2000, when for the first time the Mexican populace voted against the PRI (Revolutionary Institutionalized Party). The CEBs did not tell the members for whom they should vote, but did explain that they had been in power for seventy years and that it would be good to consider the other options.[36]

In addition to these issues on a national level, the CEBs are involved in some local programs in the parish. Every Sunday afternoon the CEBs coordinate to provide a meal for the poor children in the neighborhood. The program entitled: "Los Pobres Sirviendo Pobres" (The poor serving the poor), serves thirty to forty children, with the local units of the CEBs taking turns providing the meal every Sunday.[37] Each local unit must decide what to prepare, divide up the cost for the ingredients, and come on Sunday to cook and serve the meal. Following one meeting there was a discussion as to whether the children eating the meal were truly poor, or at least, in worse circumstances than CEB members. The group was concerned that the parents might be opportunists who were merely sending their kids for a free meal. Margarita discussed these suspicions openly with the group and assured the members that

35. Interview with Margarita, November 3, 2001.
36. Ibid.
37. Interview with Padre Bernardo, November 30, 2001.

we should not be concerned with why these children were coming for the meal, but rather just serve and trust that they were truly needy. One Sunday a month was quite frequent and the cost of providing this meal for thirty to forty children becomes a burden for the seventeen-member local unit. The members also found it more and more difficult to free up their time to cook the meal. Oftentimes one person would volunteer to cook with only two or three women coming to assist her. Nevertheless the program in the community went on and every Sunday the meal was served. But Margarita was conscious of this economic burden, because people have left the CEBs (or decided not to join) because of the constant demands.

In addition the parish also hired a physician to offer low-cost consultations and medications three days a week. Leaders of the CEBs often served as volunteer receptionists and distribute the medicine. For approximately $2.00 (U.S.) a patient could have a doctor's appointment and get a prescription, if the medicine was available at the parish. The cost of the appointment and medicine was subsidized by the parish.[38] This was made possible through donations and the purchase of government-subsidized medicines.

Among the five stages of CEB methodology (*to see, to judge, to act, to celebrate and to evaluate*) action is a key stage. Liberation theology emerged precisely as a *praxis* (action and reflection) toward the ongoing struggle (see chapter 3). While the CEBs continue to act on some issues, the level of social action does not appear to be as high as in past years. The CEB leaders often draw attention to national and international issues, however the participation of ordinary members rarely goes beyond good deeds in the community. Leaders of the CEBs have admitted that the level of commitment and involvement in national and international issues has waned since the retirement of Bishop Méndez Arceo.[39] Of course, the power shift in the Roman Catholic Church away from the CEBs has caused discouragement and fatigue in the CEB leaders, not to mention the lack of young people emerging as new leaders with creativity and energy to carry out action. Father Bernardo, current parish priest in Vista Alegre, has attributed the crisis of the CEBs to the

---

38. Private doctors in Cuernavaca usually charge between $30 and $50 (U.S.) for an appointment and filling the prescription is the responsibility of the patient.

39. Interview with Socorro Martinez, December 5, 2001.

"discouragement of not seeing new people come forward to help carry the workload."[40]

Nevertheless, the *animadores* continue to employ the methodology that has the stated learning outcome of educating and conscienticizing the members. And one cannot help but admire the long-term commitment and sacrifice of the CEB leaders who, without compensation, continue to give their time to the movement and to the service of their community. Their witness is truly an example to follow. Their concern for their neighbor at the local level is an important step toward raising consciousness among the CEB membership about national and international issues.

Summary

In summary, using the participant-observer approach I have undertaken an ethnographic study of an Ecclesial Base Community in the Colonia of Vista Alegre in Cuernavaca. I participated in pilgrimages and Bible studies, conducted interviews and questionnaires. Part of my methodology also included some quantitative research into the living conditions of the geographic region. I have learned that all the members of the local unit of the CEB are from the same rural community of Chichioalco, Guerrero. Due to droughts and economic problems members of that community migrated to Cuernavaca in search of work. Settling in the new Colonia of Vista Alegre they occupied a plot of land and began to build a home. The CEBs began in Vista Alegre in 1982, at the end of the episcopacy of Don Sergio Méndez Arceo, after many other parishes already had CEBs.

I have found that the CEBs are still a functioning network of Bible study and reflection groups. In spite of literature indicating a decline in membership, I found attendance to average eleven persons, similar to the attendance in the sixteen other local units in the parish. The CEBs consider themselves to be in crisis, since growth is stagnant and most members are between the ages of forty and sixty with little or no outreach to youth besides an occasional son or daughter in attendance. Most participants have been involved 15–20 years with little turnover in leadership positions.

40. Interview with Padre Bernardo, November 30, 2001.

The members are working poor, but over time most have been able to build a comfortable home. Remittances from adult children or relatives in the United States allow them to feel better off now than ten years ago. Family incomes range from $400 to $1,500 dollars a month, with the lower range being women without the help of additional incomes. The top leadership of the CEB has a social conscience and is concerned about national and international justice issues; but the members in attendance are not involved in social action beyond their neighborhood.

The lesson plan for the meetings is led by the *animadora* who participates in the weekly training in the parish. The purpose of the meeting is to teach the women a social consciousness through reflection on the world in light of Scripture. The content of the meeting is cognitive and analytical in nature, contrasted with spiritual and emotional. The reading and discussion skills acquired by the participants, along with the support network, allow them to feel a greater sense of self-esteem. In spite of the CEB's methodology that emphasizes praxis or reflection upon action, the social action of the CEBs rarely moves beyond good deeds.

Finally, in contrast to reports that the CEBs were disappearing, I found consistent attendance in weekly meetings and a network of "articulation" functioning. The membership is stable, but not growing and not as involved in social issues as my theoretical framework had led me to believe.

6

Ethnographic Findings of the "Discípulos de Jesus" Pentecostal Congregation in Cuernavaca

Introduction

ONLY A HALF BLOCK NORTH OF THE "NUESTRA SEÑORA DE GUADALUPE" Catholic Church, sits a large Pentecostal church which I will call "Discípulos de Jesus." A car wash is the only physical barrier that separates the two religious movements. Throughout the Colonia of Vista Alegre the members of each movement live side-by-side in the neighborhood and some have relatives in the other church. On Sunday evening, when both churches are in worship, one can even hear the Pentecostal *alabanzas* (praise music) in the distance, while attending mass in the Catholic Church. But we cannot let their geographical proximity deceive us into believing there is any cooperation between the two churches. Father Bernardo described the Pentecostal church as "ruining everything," in reference to the hegemony that the Catholic parish enjoyed up until a few years ago. Precisely because of the loud music, the Catholic Church and the neighbors filed a complaint against the Pentecostal church forcing the congregation to put up sound barriers.

Utilizing the same methodology as my field study of the CEBs, I used the participant-observer approach by participating in worship, Bible studies, retreats, and small groups, as well as conducting interviews and questionnaires to examine how this Pentecostal church related to and impacted the poor. For the purpose of my research it was important that the two movements be situated in the same *colonia*. Being located on the same block lowered the variables and margin of error in the study. While the Ecclesial Base Community I studied was recommended by a friend who had visited the local unit, *Discípulos* de Jesus was selected without any previous contact or recommendation. I attended the worship service a few times and then sought an interview with the pastor to request permission to carry out an ethnographic study. I am appreciative of his acceptance and cooperation with my research. After beginning my field work, I learned that the congregation has small cell groups called *rebaños* (which means "flock" in English) that are similar in size to a local CEB unit. While it was interesting to discover this ecclesiological parallel, my primary focus and hypothesis had to do with the relationship and impact of the Pentecostals on the poor. So I adapted my field work to include visitation of several of the *rebaños*, which will be described in this chapter.

Background of the Congregation

Discípulos began toward the end of 1993 in a private home. A young construction worker, who at the time was attending another house church, felt a "burden" to minister to the people in his own neighborhood. He began to worship in his home with his wife and eldest daughter. Soon, the congregation outgrew his living room, then his back patio, so he began looking for a vacant lot to build a place of worship. When he found one for sale, he bought half of it for himself and rented the other half for the church.

The congregational growth in numbers and resources has now produced a sprawling tabernacle the length of the property (approximately one city block). Completely self-funded, the simple cinder block construction behind a large metal front gate is unassuming, with no sign or marker distinguishing it as a church. Once inside the gate, one finds rustic outdoor bathrooms to the right and a small tin dwelling to the left that houses a family. Moving straight ahead through the dirt yard, which doubles as a small parking lot, one enters the sanctuary, which has no door for security or protection from the elements. One can walk straight through the opening in the walls to the sanctuary and eventually to the pastor's property in the back.

The sanctuary is partially covered by a tin roof that connects with a vinyl tent-like shelter to protect the sanctuary from the elements. The floor is laid block that slants down from the back wall to the altar. Hundreds of plastic chairs in rows fill the sanctuary. The altar, looking more like an outdoor stage at the county fairgrounds, is equally rustic with cement steps on either side leading up to the pulpit. The musical instruments—drum set, electric guitar and piano—are to the right, and four chairs for the pastor, lay liturgist and distinguished guests to the left. On the back wall of the chancel hang several red banners with shinny gold letters which read: "Admirable, Consejero, Dios Fuerte, Padre Eterno, Principe de Paz, Jésus" (Admirable, Counselor, Strong God, Eternal Father, Prince of Peace, Jesus). A large amplifier sits on the stage with several large speakers surrounding the altar. An inadequate number of fluorescent lights hang from the roof.

Two side walls protect the property from the adjacent lots, but the front and the back walls were erected only after the neighbors—largely spurred on by the Catholic Church—filed a complaint with the local municipality for violation of noise ordinances. On one Sunday when I was in attendance, the pastor announced: "We need the help of a few volunteers tomorrow because we have to build a wall here." I could not come, but the following Sunday the wall was complete. Later, in a private interview with the pastor, I learned that the wall was built to comply with the noise complaint filed by the Catholic Church.[1] Behind the newly erected wall toward the back of the property are two classrooms and the pastor's office, which is simple and clean with a desk, computer, bookcase and two chairs for visitors. Plans are in place to build a second floor of classrooms above the present structure. At the very back of the property (facing the next street) the pastor has begun a two-story parsonage for his family which is still unfinished.

Life Story of Pastor Silvero Montero

Born in 1950 in the city of Altimirano, Guerrero, Silverio Montero (not his real name) was the fourteenth of eighteen children. His father was a peasant and worked in the fields to feed his family. Silverio was brought to Cuernavaca to live with relatives when he was seven because his parents did not earn enough to support him. He remembers crying himself to sleep as a child and feeling as though his parents did not love him. Now that he is older, however, he realizes how much it costs to feed and clothe a child and no longer harbors resentment. He was raised by another family and had to work as a young age. Today Pastor Montero

1. Interview with Pastor Silverio Montero, May 30, 2002.

shares his personal testimony as an example of how God has a purpose for us:

> When I was seven years-old my parents brought me and my three younger brothers to Cuernavaca. We were like a staircase in ages—four, five, six and seven. We were a large family and it was difficult for my parents to feed us all. If you have a family of five and have one more kid, then you can just add more water to the soup. But when you have eighteen kids it is impossible to feed them all. So they brought us to Cuernavaca to enroll my three younger brothers in a children's home. My brothers didn't want to stay. The first few nights were very painful. The oldest of the three, Juan, tried to act like the little man. He told the other two: "Don't cry! Boys don't cry." But then when the other two fell asleep, Juan started crying. Nevertheless as we grew up, we saw the hand of God in our lives. God had a plan for us. Now all of us are evangelicals; that probably wouldn't have happened if we would have stayed with my parents.[2]

After moving to Cuernavaca as a child, Silverio grew up in the nearby working class neighborhood of Carolina where he learned to play baseball. Gifted at sports, he played on a baseball team throughout his youth, until joining a semi-professional team as a young adult. Playing baseball provided an emotional release from the pain of his childhood. He became very close to his teammates and they were almost like family for him. Even after getting a job in construction, he continued to play and hang out with the guys. Following the games he often went out drinking with them, and prided himself on picking up the bar tab. Pastor Silverio recalls:

> If before I was proud to invite my friends out to drink and pay the tab, even more now I should be proud to give my offering to God. Sometimes I would go out and drink and not remember what I did. Then the next morning I would wake up with a hangover, open my wallet and think "What did I do?" But if my pride pushed me to pay the bill, then now for God, I should be even more proud to give a generous offering to God.[3]

Silverio learned the construction business well and after making some contacts he decided to start a contracting firm. He bid on remod-

2. Recorded from Pastor Montero's sermon.

3. Ibid; my translation.

eling, painting and construction jobs and supervised his workers. He ran a successful business, played semi-professional baseball, and went back to school to finish middle school. After marrying and having his first daughter, Silverio experienced a personal crisis:

> My wife was pregnant with our second child when she presented signs of a miscarriage. At that time my god was money. I thought that if I had enough money I could buy anything I wanted—including the best medical care. So I took my wife to the best hospital in Cuernavaca and expected her pregnancy to be saved. She was hospitalized for a few days and then the doctor said she was free to go. I thought everything would be fine. That same night she woke up with pains in her abdomen and miscarried the child. I didn't know where to turn. My brother spoke to me saying that when all the medical care fails, God is the doctor above all doctors. I told him that I had my religion (Roman Catholicism) and that I respected his religion (Protestantism) and he should respect mine. He dialogued with me some more, but I was very stubborn. So he just suggested I read my Bible. I had a Bible, but I had never read it. I opened it up and the Word of God began to speak to me. With my brother's prodding, I converted on my own.[4]

After this experience, Silverio began visiting a Pentecostal mission in another neighborhood with his brother, where he attended for about nine months. Dissatisfied with the lay pastor of that house church, Silverio felt a "burden" for his own neighborhood: Colonia Alta Vista Alegre. He felt that the church could be growing faster, so he began to hold worship services with his wife and children in his own home. Gradually inviting neighbors and relatives, the group met in his living room and then moved to the back patio. Montero then had a vision of buying a plot of land for the church, but wanted property facing Vista Alegre's main street. When a lot became available he sold all of his other properties in order to buy half the lot. He rented the rest in the name of the church and together with the congregation built a temporary tin-roof church structure.

---

4. Interview with Silverio Montero, May 30, 2002; my translation.

Ecclesial Church Structure

Although the pastor, a former construction worker, started the congregation and built the facilities with the help of the congregation, this work is part of a larger growth strategy of a Pentecostal Church in the United States. According to Nida's typology of indigenous churches in Latin America, *Discípulos* would be considered a "mission-front" church,[5] which is financially solvent, but enjoys only partial autonomy. *Discípulos* is part of a larger worldwide denominational structure with offices in Mexico City and mission headquarters in the United States.[6] This particular denomination, which I will call Pentecostal Church U.S.A., has been working in Mexico for twenty years. It was founded in 1945 in the United States as the result of a merger between two "oneness" Pentecostal organizations[7]—one of which traces its roots back to the Pentecostal revival of Charles Parham in 1901. It is a large denomination that has an international mission wing which oversees work in 148 countries throughout the world, and four missionaries assigned to Mexico. One of the missionaries was transferred from Central America to Mexico twelve years ago to assume the supervision of the Mexico mission work. Under his leadership the denomination has grown from twenty to 400 churches throughout Mexico. *Discípulos* de Jesus is one of those new church starts, which has, in turn, started several missions on its own.

Internally, *Discípulos* is governed by an executive committee made up of eight lay leaders and the pastor. While the senior pastor is officially called the general pastor, the lay leaders are also called pastors of different ministries, including youth pastor, administrative pastor and regional cell group pastors (in Spanish *pastores de rebaños* which literally means "shepherds of the flock"). The executive committee meets once a month to govern the church body. In addition there are 18 *pastores de rebaños* who meet on Monday evenings to prepare for the house-church meetings during the week. While all of the executive committee members are men, approximately half of the pastors of *re-*

5. Nida, "Indigenous Churches in Latin America," 97–105. See a description of Nida's typologies on 19.

6. I have chosen not to reveal the name of the denomination to respect the anonymity of the congregation per request of the pastor.

7. Oneness churches, often called "apostolic," believe that Jesus is the Father and reject the doctrine of the Trinity.

baños are women. Both men and women have their own organizations which meet separately. The women meet every Thursday for a worship service and afterwards have a general business meeting. The men meet only occasionally. The women contribute greatly to fundraising efforts of the church while the men help in construction projects. The youth also have a separate organization for adolescents ages twelve and up. Once married, couples leave the youth organization and join the men's and women's organizations. The church also has a Sunday school program for children during the worship service, and once a month the children have their own "children's church."

Discípulos has a congregation of four hundred baptized members, an average worship attendance of three hundred, and thirty *rebaños* that meet in private homes for Bible study throughout Cuernavaca. Some of those in the *rebaños* also attend the mother church, but most are new converts beginning to learn about the faith. The church activities at *Discípulos* include Sunday afternoon worship, Monday meeting for *rebaño* pastors, Wednesday evening Bible study, Thursday women's meeting, Friday youth meeting, and Saturday praise service. The other evenings are free for the people to attend a *rebaño*. In addition to this local outreach in Cuernavaca, sixteen new mission churches have emerged out of this mother church, which has trained, sent, and partially financed pastors to work in towns throughout the states of Morelos and Guerrero.

Composition of *Discípulos*

The make-up of the congregation is diverse in terms of gender and age. Of the adults surveyed in the respective men's and women's organizations, 34 percent were young people between twenty and thirty. The age groups 30–39 and 40–49 each were 21 percent, with ages 50–60 a mere 11 percent, with the remainder being over sixty. These figures indicate that the congregation is fairly well balanced age-wise. The gender composition of the congregation is 57 percent women and 43 percent men, with many young couples and families. The average nuclear family is made up of 4.3 members. There is also a large youth group and children's program. The overwhelming majority of the adults are married with only a few being single, widowed or divorced. On Fridays the youth organize their own worship service with an average attendance of forty. On Sundays there is an average of thirty-five children in Sunday school.

Thirty-one percent of the congregation is originally from Cuernavaca while the other 69 percent percent have migrated from other neighboring states such as Guerrero. Surprisingly, those who have migrated have now lived in Cuernavaca an average of twenty years. Eighty percent of the congregation live in Vista Alegre and walk to church. The church has a small parking lot, but there are usually only two or three cars parked there on Sunday. This indicates either that people live within walking distance of the church or take public transportation. Thirty-nine percent of the adults interviewed have finished at least middle school, with only 11 percent completing high school. Seventy-four percent had finished at least primary school, with only 5 percent not having any schooling and being illiterate. Construction worker was the most prominent occupation of the men, while housewife and domestic worker were the most often mentioned for the women. Other occupations of the men were: electrician, plumber, welder, waiter, gardener, vender, taxi driver, mechanic, government office worker and military. Fifty-four percent of those responding to the questionnaire indicated an income equivalent to $200–$400 a month. Only 8 percent reported an income between $400 and $600 a month with all others earning $200 or less. In spite of these low figures, 79 percent perceive themselves to be economically equal to others in the community, and the overwhelming majority (87 percent) of the members report being better off financially than before their conversion. Fifty-one percent of those responding either rent or are building their own home. The rest either own their own home or live with family.

The results of the questionnaire indicate that the *Discípulos* congregation is mostly made up of working-class immigrants from neighboring states. Slightly more than half are either renting or building their own homes. There is a slight gender difference with more women than men. Many women attend alone or with their children, but there is a strong representation of young families in which the husband does accompany his wife. In spite of the number of youth and young families every age group is well represented.

Description of the Pentecostal Gathering

The principal gathering of the week is Sunday worship at 4:00 PM on Sunday afternoons—which is significant because this is an important family gathering time in Mexican culture.[8] Actually starting closer to 5:00, the congregation gradually gathers while a youth praise band leads loud Christian praise songs from the chancel. Two greeters stand at the doorway to shake hands and show visitors to their seats. First-time guests are given an attendance card to supply their name and address. The members arrive alone or with their families and often first go to the altar to pray or kneel at their seats. After a brief prayer they stand and join in the singing that could last as long as an hour before the formal welcome and start of the program.

Around 6:00 a lay liturgist (called a deacon) seated on the stage comes forward to the pulpit, offers a few words of exhortation, and asks the congregation to be seated. He then proceeds to welcome the congregation and read off the names of visitors from the attendance cards. These guests are asked to stand and be welcomed by the congregation with a round of applause. The congregation is then invited to stand for the reading of a Bible passage. Sometimes the deacon reads the passage alone and other times he will ask the congregation to read alternate verses. The praise band plays another set of more intense praise music picking up the tempo. At this point the service has been going over an hour and the pastor has yet to appear.

During this second set of praise songs the pastor usually appears in the back of the sanctuary, walks up to the stage and stands alongside the lay liturgist to the left of the pulpit. After another twenty minutes of enthusiastic singing, the pastor approaches the pulpit, asks the congregation to be seated, and gives the announcements about upcoming events, meetings, retreats, and fundraising drives. Compared to the uneasiness of the lay liturgist, the pastor has an authoritative, commanding, and polished voice. The congregation listens attentively, nods affirmatively, and after an exhortation responds vocally with a spontaneous *"Amen!"* *"Gloria a Dios!"* or *"Alleluia!"* Following the announcements, the pastor invites the deacons to come forward with the offering plates. The con-

---

8. It is very common for extended family to gather on Sunday afternoons in traditional Mexican culture. Adult children who are married and live on their own often return on Sundays to visit their parents.

gregation stands and the praise band sings a couple of songs while the offering is being collected. After the songs the ushers come forward for the pastor to bless the offering. The praise band then begins a third set of enthusiastic praise music. The congregation joins in and the pastor concludes his final exhortation and sings with the crowd. The congregation seemingly recharges its energy from the pastor's contagious enthusiasm and stands to join in the praise music. This time the tempo picks up and people begin to dance in their seats. As the music gets faster and faster, a buzz seems to fill the air. Some people move out into the aisles and dance down to the open space in front of the altar. Some kneel to pray, others enter a state of ecstasy as they jump, dance and run around the sanctuary. Yet others turn to the outside walls and raise their hands as if to be in their own private communion with God. Some begin to frantically wave their arms, cry and scream as they stand in their place. From Sunday to Sunday the intensity, enthusiasm and duration of the praise time vary, but the volume of the music is always loud, especially near the front. As the level of energy in the sanctuary heightens, the service seems to be building up to a climax.

The pastor approaches the pulpit and the stage is set. He plays upon the enthusiasm of the congregation and invokes the name of Jesus like a motivational speaker at a pep rally. Finally, the pastor opens his Bible and invites the congregation to follow along in the reading, which is rarely longer than two or three verses. Sometimes he invites the congregation to read the passage in unison or responsively in alternating verses. The pastor then prays over the passage and invites the people to be seated. At this time he invites the children to go to their Sunday school and the thirty to forty children, previously hidden in the sea of blue chairs, work their way through the aisles to their classrooms.

The pastor's sermons are enthusiastic, colorful, and anecdotal. He commands center stage. His animated preaching style and cordless microphone allow him to wave his hands and wander the entire stage. He illustrates the sermon with body language; sometimes skillfully impersonating the voice of a drunk or mimicking persons using common street language. The powerful amplifier allows his voice to fill the sanctuary and it can be heard as far as a block away. As he comes back to the pulpit he glances at his notes and occasionally reads a quote or definition of a Greek term. He always announces a sermon title and begins on this topic. More often than not, however, he departs from his notes and spontaneously uses illustrations from real life experiences.

On one occasion he preached about Jesus Christ being the corner-stone of our faith and gave illustrations based on his experience in the construction business. In another sermon he spoke of a Christian re-turning to his former worldly lifestyle like a newly-bathed pig waddling in the mud. These illustrations come from his life experience and relate to the rural and working-class roots of the congregation. Throughout the sermon the congregation participates with spontaneous shouts of *"Amen!" "Gloria a Dios!"* and *"Alleluia!"* Occasionally they stand, raise their hands and applaud with approval. The sermon builds in intensity and creates anticipation for the climax. The pastor's voice gets louder and more enthusiastic. Toward the end of the sermon the crowd stands and enters into frenzy.

The stage is now set for the altar call. The praise band begins to play softly in the background while the pastor invites all those, depending on the subject of the sermon, who would like to heal their pain, resent-ment, or anger, or let go of some behavior, to come down to the chancel. It is not necessarily an invitation for new believers, but an invitation for an encounter with the divine. Mostly women approach at first, to be fol-lowed by young men, and eventually the majority of the congregation. The large open space in front of the altar is filled with people kneeling, standing and sprawling on the floor. The rest of the congregation re-mains standing, singing and praying in their seats. Some kneel in their places while others stand and raise their hands as the pastor and the deacons pray for each individual at the altar. The intensity of this altar call varies from Sunday to Sunday with manifestations of crying, trem-bling and screaming. The collective effect of the many voices crying and screaming creates a high-pitched commotion in the sanctuary with the praise band playing softly in the background.

The altar call is the climax toward which the whole worship ser-vice and sermon have been building. This is the moment of encounter with the divine that is encouraged throughout the Pentecostal wor-ship experience. To the casual visitor who is not used to a Pentecostal worship style, the altar call may appear to be chaotic. Nevertheless, over the course of several Sundays, I realized that the altar call was quite routine and orderly. Only on one occasion did I witness people being "slain in the Spirit" (falling), and surprisingly on only one occasion did I witness somebody speaking in tongues. After a brief time of prayer and singing at the altar the people one-by-one return to their seats and continue to sing.

Following the altar call is a hallowing silence—the first since the service began—broken only by the laughter of children returning to the congregation from their classrooms. There is a sense of relief or peace following the discharge of so much energy. The pastor, who was down off the stage praying and laying his hands on people, returns to the pulpit to announce one more song. Occasionally the pastor or the song leader will have a final reminder of a pending announcement like: "The youth will be meeting briefly after the service;" or "Today there will be baptisms after the service and all are welcome." Then the music stops and the people turn to greet their neighbors as they head for the exit. Bibles, Christian literature and refreshments are for sale as people greet each other on the way to the door. Members usually linger for several minutes in the churchyard while visiting with their friends.

Another important activity of *Discípulos* is the weekly meetings of *rebaños* in private homes. Not all Pentecostal churches have cell groups, and I was not aware that *Discípulos* did until I had a preliminary interview with Pastor Montero and he showed me a three dimensional model he had on his desk. Looking like a high school physics model of the solar system, this showed the mother church with one big yellow ball in the center, surrounded by medium-sized red balls (*rebaños*), which were, in turn, surrounded by several smaller blue balls representing the cell group members. The *rebaños* meet once a week in private homes and are strategically located to attract more people to the mother church. This church growth strategy had the vision of reaching across Cuernavaca, but at the time nearly all the cell groups were located in the immediate vicinity of Vista Alegre. In addition, on the back wall of the sanctuary there was a large map of Cuernavaca with red dots indicating the location of the *rebaños.*

The cell group church growth strategy has been around since the Primitive Church, but Pastor Montero acted as though he had invented it. He showed me a booklet that he wrote to train the *pastores de rebaño*, which presented an evangelism strategy with several Bible lessons. In addition to this initial training seminar, the pastor offers ongoing training for the *pastores de rebaño*. While he travels around to visit them occasionally, it is largely the responsibility of the lay leader to make them grow. The lay people who oversee this ministry usually lead two or three *rebaños* without compensation in addition to other responsibilities in the church.

I visited several *rebaños* during my field work and what follows is a description of one meeting. Pastor Montero recommended that I visit this particular *rebaño* (I believe as a gesture of support) which was located in a rural area outside Cuernavaca in a heavily Roman Catholic community that was known for persecuting evangelicals. I recorded the following in my field notes:

> We traveled outside of Cuernavaca to a ranch of a wealthy Mexican actor. Our host received us at the gate and showed us to the care-taker's house where he stayed. Around 7:30 PM the other participants began to arrive—a total of eleven adults [six men and five women] and five children—not including myself and Antonio. Five of those in attendance were related as the daughter of the caretaker; her husband and five year-old daughter were also present. We entered the caretaker's house which consisted of two rooms—a bedroom with two single beds and a dresser, and a kitchen/dining room area where Janet took the five children. As the adults assembled in the bedroom I could easily hear her singing, playing games and talking in the other room through the cardboard walls. Antonio led the service, which included a Bible reading, singing, prayer, testimonies and a sermon. Antonio preached a short biblically-based exhortation from the Letter to the Ephesians. I could deduce from the context of the sermon and the testimonies that the evangelicals in this region were a small minority who felt ostracized. One woman shared how the local school charged a compulsive fee per child to cover the cost of the fiesta for the patron saint. She discussed her dilemma of paying it and the real risk of not paying. The worship ended with a time of fellowship while hot *atole*[9] and sweet bread were served.

This work of Antonio and Janet is bearing fruit as this small cell group has grown in very hostile territory. They usually go on the bus and take a taxi home after dark. Antonio even makes a second trip out to the mission on Tuesday nights for a prayer service just with adults. The pastor shared with me how difficult it has been to sustain the work in that region as the believers often face persecution and become dis-

9. *Atole* is a typical Mexican drink that is made from corn and has a thick consistency.

couraged. By this time Antonio and Janet had been able to maintain a nucleus of believers for several months, who travel into Cuernavaca (a 45-minute trip by car) every Sunday afternoon for the principal worship service at Discípulos.

The Teachings of the *Discípulos*

Although the *Discípulos* congregation refers to the Bible as the central authority for Christian doctrine, the passages read in worship are usually short and rarely analyzed in depth. Passages such as Matt 9:20 about the woman suffering from twelve years of hemorrhaging and Matt 21:42 describing "the stone that the builders rejected becoming the cornerstone," are read frequently. These and other similar passages highlight the theme of redemption for the poor and marginalized of society. In the latter, Jesus Christ himself was rejected yet became the foundation for the Kingdom of God.

Another genre of Scripture common in sermons and Bible studies emphasizes the omnipotence of God. Passages such as Psalm 84 and Isa 33:23 describe God as ruler or king. In more than one sermon the pastor has compared God's power to the limited power of worldly rulers as an illustration to show how much more powerful God is. This is reassuring to the congregation who has faith that God will protect God's children. Adjectives such as big, strong and giant are often used to describe the almighty God. Theologically, the Pentecostal doctrine emphasizes the theistic God as omnipotent, omnipresent, and omniscient. Emphasizing the omnipotence of the divine usually implies the weakness of humans. However, Pastor Silverio has also preached on the importance of human initiative in faith, receiving the Holy Spirit, and perseverance in sanctification.

Pastor Silverio often reads Luke 4:18–19 to emphasize the work of the Holy Spirit: "The Spirit of the Lord is upon me, because he has anointed me to bring good news to the poor. He has sent me to proclaim release to the captives and recovery of sight to the blind, to let the oppressed go free, to proclaim the year of the Lord's favor." In his sermons the pastor emphasizes how the Holy Spirit has chosen each individual for a specific purpose. This theology encourages people, especially the marginalized people in the working class Colonia de Vista Alegre, to believe that they are special as children of God sealed by the Holy Spirit.

Another important theme for *Discípulos* is baptism and new birth. When Jesus instructed Nicodemus on how to enter the kingdom of God he said: "Very truly, I tell you, no one can enter the kingdom of God without being born of water and Spirit."[10] The passage in Acts 2:36–38 emphasizes both repentance and baptism. Pastor Silverio teaches that sin must die in order for the person to be reborn. Baptism is an outward sign of an inward change. According to the pastor, one must be baptized in order to be saved. The only acceptable form of baptism is immersion. There is a baptistery in the back of the church which always contains water. Nearly every other Sunday there are one or two people who decide to be baptized—apparently spontaneously. The pastor or one of the deacons may baptize a convert following the service after a brief explanation of its meaning. Pastor Silverio teaches that "to baptize" in Greek also means to submerge. Therefore sprinkling is not acceptable. Neither baptisms from the Roman Catholic Church, nor from any Trinitarian Protestant church are recognized.[11]

Although the pastor emphasizes the importance of baptism for salvation, water baptism is not equated or simultaneous with baptism of the Holy Spirit. This distinct experience is called the doctrine of the "second blessing." Pentecostals emphasize a second saving experience in addition to water baptism in which one receives the Holy Spirit and is sealed for salvation: "The [Pentecostal Church U.S.A.] distinguishes itself from other Pentecostal groups in that we firmly believe that receiving the Holy Spirit is for all. It is not merely optional, but something that all can and should receive."[12] This doctrine is so important for the Pentecostal Church U.S.A. that the church keeps separate categories of statistics for the number baptized and the number who have received the Holy Spirit.

A doctrine taught by the Pentecostal Church U.S.A. is the "oneness" or unity of Jesus Christ. While not uncommon, this doctrine is only taught in a minority of Pentecostal churches.[13] Based on a few passages such as Acts 2:38 calling for baptism in the name of Jesus

10. John 3:5.

11. Since baptism in the Roman Catholic Church is not accepted by Pastor Silverio, he does not believe that Catholics will be saved unless they repent, are baptized and receive the Holy Spirit in an oneness Pentecostal church.

12. Drost, *Fueron Todos Llenos*, 2.

13. See n. 7 above.

Christ, this non-Trinitarian doctrine states that Jesus is the Father and the Holy Spirit.[14] In a Bible study entitled *"Quien era Jesucristo?"* (Who was Jesus Christ?) Pastor Silverio supported this doctrine largely with passages such as "The Father and I are one" (John 10:30) and "Whoever has seen me has seen the Father" (John 14:8–9). This doctrine illustrates the sectarian or exclusivist attitude of the *Discípulos* church that does not recognize Trinitarian baptisms. Even other Pentecostals, who were baptized in the name of the Trinity, must be re-baptized in the name of Jesus to become a member of the church.

Hymnology

The songs of *Discípulos* also emphasize the centrality and power of Jesus as divine. Music is a major part of Pentecostal worship, as we saw in the previous section, praise songs occupy about two-thirds of the worship service. Participants do not seem to mind standing and singing repetitive choruses for as long as thirty minutes at a time. On the contrary, singing energizes the congregation. Also the praise band plays music in the background during the altar call which facilitates an encounter with the divine.

The members of the praise band, who are called *levitas*, must have a proven moral conduct before being allowed to join. The group practices once a week and plays in all the services during the week. This is a significant time commitment, but it is considered a privilege to belong. In fact, there were so many youth wanting to join that the church formed two praise bands which alternate Sundays. Both bands have a drummer, electric guitarist, bass player, and usually three female background singers. The guitarists and bass players are all males, but there is one female drummer who alternates Sundays. They range in ages between sixteen and twenty-three years old. None of the members have studied music professionally, but they have learned to play by ear.

Alberto, the pastor's nephew, is the leader of the praise band and usually is the lead guitarist and singer as well. He has the responsibility of organizing the band and choosing the songs. The pastor may censor the songs or make requests, but Alberto has grown up in the church

---

14. This has similarities to the third- and fourth-century heresies of Monarchism and Sabellianism (modalism). These heresies state that the divine is able to manifest itself in any of the three modes or forms.

and is very close emotionally and theologically to the pastor. He senses when to start playing a song as the pastor is concluding his sermon, and spontaneously at other points in the service. From my vantage point there does not appear to be any planned order or timing. The pastor does not seem to be upset by these interruptions and goes with the music. The central role of music in the service gives these young people, particularly Alberto, a great deal of visibility and power.

The songs are repetitive choruses which are easy to remember. Most people seem to memorize them quickly as the church does not have any hymnals or an LCD projector. One popular song refers to Jesus as the King:

> Let's praise the King
> Let's all praise the King
>
> Every knee shall bow
> Every tongue confess that
> Jesus Christ is the Lord;
> Jesus Christ is the Savior
>
> I will exalt your name
> Oh, highest one
>
> In that name there is power
> And that name is Jesus
>
> Jesus![15]

This song incorporates the early Christian hymn in Phil 2:10–11 with the Pentecostal emphasis on Jesus as King. The name of Jesus is exalted as having power as Lord and Savior.

Another popular song emphasizes the power of praising Jesus over the forces of evil. This may be popular to the amount of injustice and evil that the members face in their daily lives. The lyrics are:

> We will destroy forts in the world in the name of Jesus.
> If you want to have this power, all you have to do is praise him
> Take your instrument, all your armor, you are powerful in God.
> Here is the power in God
>
> You have the power,
> I have the power,
> We have the power of God.[16]

15. As recorded during a worship service at *Discípulos*.
16. Ibid.

This song emphasizes the power in the act of praising Jesus. The people appear to be comforted by a powerful Jesus in contrast to the powerlessness that they experience in their daily lives. When one praises Jesus one obtains power over the evil "forts."

The lyrics of the praise songs are easy to memorize and repeat. The music itself is loud, enthusiastic and contagious. The majority of the congregation seems to have memorized the lyrics and sing along joyfully. The melody is *allegre* and spirit-filled. The theology is dualistic, with images of good, light, power, big, and king for Jesus against the evil forces of darkness in this world. The congregation is invited to participate in this power through praise and saying the name of Jesus, and this gives them at least a temporary sense of relief from the sometime overwhelming circumstances of their everyday lives.

Leadership and Empowerment

The leadership model presented by Pastor Silverio Montero can be characterized as charismatic and authoritarian. He encourages new members to assume responsibility and become active in evangelization and discipleship, but maintains a centralized authority and control over major decisions. He chairs the executive committee and is the central figure in worship. The treasury is handled by another man, but the pastor seems to keep a close watch on how funds are used. The only elections held are for the officers of the men's, women's and youth organizations of the church. While lay people can take initiative and show creativity as *pastores de rebaño*, he teaches their training seminar. Members of the congregation may feel like chosen children of God and empowered toward a sense of dignity and self-worth, however their ability to develop freedom of expression and critical thinking may be inhibited by the authoritarian leadership of the pastor.

Women are well represented as pastors of the *rebaños*, participate in fund-raising, and volunteer for special events, however they do not preach or lead worship services unless it is a women's service. In addition women make up a majority of the congregation and participate in different aspects of the church life. The participation of women is even more impressive when one realizes the sacrifice one must make to be active in church. Twenty-five percent of the women report some type of criticism of their church participation from their husbands, yet 70%

attend almost all of the church activities. Apparently women feel some sense of validation which sustains their involvement in church activities. In spite of being in the majority, women are limited in their public leadership roles.

The questionnaire also revealed that members of the congregation appear to experience positive changes in their lives upon beginning their association with *Discípulos*. The participants reported major improvements in their family life and marriage after coming to the church. In many cases there was some type of crisis, such as a bout with alcoholism, marital problems, a life-threatening illness, or a death in the family that preceded their decision to come to church. Most participants were non-practicing Roman Catholics and were invited to *Discípulos* by a friend, family member or colleague from work. Thirty-three percent reported a general improvement in their life after coming to church. All of the participants in the survey reported have some type of "conversion" experience and were baptized at *Discípulos*. Some respondents were more specific as to the fruits of their conversion citing reconciliation in their marriages, family unification or a healing experience. The most frequent improvement in the quality of life, especially among men, was abstinence from alcohol. Interestingly, women reported the abstinence of their husbands to be the biggest improvement in their own lives. Stories like that of María are common, which suggests that women feel a positive change and are empowered by their church involvement.

María is one of the lay pastors of the *rebaño* groups. Being Catholic until four years ago, it had never occurred to her to become evangelical. María moved to Cuernavaca from a small town in Guerrero ten years ago. The transition to the city was very difficult. Her husband found work as a gardener in the homes of a few wealthy families. He worked long hours, taking on extra gardens in order to buy construction materials to build their home. Gardening for wealthy families was hard denigrating work, but paid much better than farming in his hometown. María stayed at home to care for the children, but found the behavior and values that they brought home from school to be very different from how she had been raised. With no extended family around, she often felt lonely and isolated. Having attended mass in her home town, she found consolation in reading the Scriptures. One day about four years ago a neighbor invited her to *Discípulos*. She was very antagonistic toward evangelicals (or *alleluias* as they are called derogatorily) and was resistant at first. However, feeling the need for contact with other people, a sense of community, and a break in her lonely routine at home, she finally agreed.

Upon arriving at the church one Sunday, María's initial impression of *Discípulos* was that it was loud and unruly. She just looked around in amazement at the emotional outbursts as people closed their eyes, sang and danced to the music. María recalls:

> I was taught as a girl that church was a solemn place of worship. I went to mass and was very reverent. I repeated the Prayer of Jesus and the Hail Mary, but it was more of a routine. I didn't listen to the words I was saying or feel God's presence. The Pentecostal Church is very different. I found people to be alive and they welcomed me with a smile. In the Catholic Church people attend mass as a requirement, but don't live their faith. In the Pentecostal Church the people believe in Jesus and are encouraged to feel and experience the Holy Spirit. Now I feel the confirmation that Jesus is in my life and helping me.[17]

María had always been a very quiet and unassuming person. She had stayed at home to raise her children and had never been involved in any type of public engagement. However, her lifestyle changed two years ago. After only being Protestant two years, the pastor asked her if she would host a Bible study in her home. She felt inadequate since she was new herself. The pastor asked her to pray about it and discern what God was leading her to do. María did have lots of relatives in the neighborhood that had moved from Guerrero. Her son, Gabriel, did play the guitar and could assist her with the music. But she was a shy person who was not sure if she had the ability. Finally, she felt God encouraging her to begin this new ministry and the pastor said that he would provide her with training and support.

María began with her son and daughter and two nieces. She decided that in order to attract more people, it would be better to host the meeting in her niece's house to evangelize her family. After a slow start during which she sometimes considered giving up, the *rebaño* began to attract more members of her extended family and a few neighbors. Her parents, who had been staunch Catholics in Guerrero, even began to attend. Most of the resistance came from her husband. He accused her of abandoning the home and the children and threatened to leave

17. Interview with María Morales, June 16, 2002; my translation.

her. In response, María tried to keep the Bible studies short so as not to get home too late. The newly-found community sustained her during these difficult times, and the new leadership role and positive results encouraged her to keep on. She felt as though she was gaining a new-found sense of purpose and self-worth. One Friday she asked Pastor Silverio to lead the Bible study because she felt that several of the new converts were ready for baptism. I attended this meeting and recorded the following in my field notes:

> I arrived a little late at 5:15, but nobody had arrived except for María. She invited me to have a seat in the living room, but said that the Bible study would be held in the back patio. Gradually, other friends and relatives began to arrive and María's niece escorted us to the patio. Pastor Silverio arrived and greeted everyone by name. The group consisted of 12 adults—nine women and three men. María began leading the group with a couple of praise songs accompanied by her son on the guitar. I was happy to see a collection of song sheets was available for guests who did not know the words. Then María invited the pastor to lead the study. He asked if there was any particular topic they wanted to discuss and María said baptism. Pastor Silverio began an hour-long Bible study on baptism citing John 3:1–6 and Acts 2:38. He appeared to be spontaneous with no notes, but seemed very well rehearsed with Bible passages. He assigned Scriptural passages and invited the participants to look them up in their Bibles. He was very persuasive, but paused periodically to allow time for any questions. At the end of the study the participants were quite convinced of their need for repentance and new birth. The study concluded with prayer about 9:00pm. I thanked María and Pastor Silverio for the invitation to attend, greeted all those present, and walked back to my car only to discover that my hubcaps had been stolen.[18]

The Sunday following the Bible study several of those in attendance, including six of María's relatives, asked to be baptized. Later that month María was named the "*Pastor de Rebaño*" of the month.

Social Action and Political Involvement

I was only aware of two social programs that the *Discípulos* offered in the community. One was a food basket to which members of the church

18. Field notes, June 14, 2002.

contributed staple foods (rice, beans and canned goods), and once a month the church distributed the food to elderly and needy families in the community. Usually the recipients were related somehow to the congregation, although the pastor announced that distribution was not conditional upon attendance at the church.

One Sunday the pastor announced the new program: "This week a woman from the SEP [Secretary of Public Education] came to the church and offered free elementary and secondary school classes in exchange for using our space. I readily agreed and would like to encourage all of you who have not yet had the opportunity to continue your education to do so." The second social program was loaning their space for adults seeking to complete their elementary and secondary education. The program continues in the church with an average attendance of nine adults.

Other social outreach continues at the individual and private level through personal and family contacts in the neighborhood. Bible studies and sermons emphasize the example of Jesus and the social ethics of the gospel. Members are encouraged not to be selfish and to share with their neighbor.

Although members of the church are poor, 75 percent of those surveyed considered themselves to be at the same economic as those surrounding them in the community. This was intended to be a very subjective question which would reveal more about one's attitude toward one's relative well-being than about the hard economic statistics of one's income. Only 16 percent of those who responded considered themselves to be worse off than others in the community. However, in reality the members interviewed had a monthly household income between the equivalent of U.S. $200–$400.[19] This perceived equality can be seen as a positive sense of dignity and self-worth, which has replaced self-pity.

The questionnaire also revealed a lack of interest and involvement in public politics. Half of the adults participating indicated that they never watched the news on television or read the newspaper. Although the congregation clearly affirmed their right and obligation as citizens to vote in elections (87 percent), they were nearly equally divided in their preferences for the three major political parties in Mexico (PAN,

19. Questionnaire conducted among the CEB members.

PRI, and PRD).[20] Although they were in favor of voting, the question-niaire reveals that they were not knowledgeable about the recent conflicts in the state of Chiapas between the Zapatistas and the Mexican government. On the local level, however, they did feel that they should be of service to others.

Summary

The *Discípulos* de Jesus congregation began as a house church in the home of Pastor Silverio Montero and, in only ten years, had grown to a congregation of four hundred people with thirty-five *rebaño* groups meeting in private homes. While maintaining a relationship to the mother church in the United States, *Discípulos* was largely autonomous and had started sixteen mission churches on its own.

The membership composition of *Discípulos* was just shy of two-thirds women and was well-balanced with respect to age. Most of the members had migrated to Cuernavaca from other states, but they had an average of twenty years living in the city—although not necessarily in Vista Alegre. The members worked in a variety of professions, but were predominantly working-class—the average years of schooling were very low. The Pentecostal families reported an average income between U.S. $200 and $400 a month. Most of the adult members were not home owners—thus making them vulnerable to moving a lot.

Sunday worship was the principal gathering and was a very joyous and boisterous activity. The music, Scripture readings and sermon all led up to the climatic altar call, which, in the words of Pastor Montero, fulfilled the objective of worship of facilitating an encounter with the divine. Although this emotional experience often produced a feeling of ecstasy, the intellectual development of the members helped them understand the significance of their faith. Worship, in addition to Bible study, promoted baptism and new birth as essential for salvation. Unique to this denomination was the "oneness" non-Trinitarian doctrine of baptism in the name of Jesus. The hymns reflected the centrality of Jesus and utilized the images of "king" and as powerful. This

---

20. The PAN (National Action Party) has a conservative *laissez faire* platform. The PRI (Institutionalized Revolutionary Party) represents the interests of the status quo and had ruled since the aftermath of Mexican Revolution in 1919. The PRD (Revolutionary Democratic Party) is the most progressive and nationalistic of the main parties.

may have emerged from their context of powerlessness in the midst of everyday situations of injustice and evil.

As the individuals in the congregation have entered this Pentecostal Church, they have found a new support community. Following upon crisis and poverty, people have come together to find a new sense of purpose and meaning in their lives. In spite of an authoritarian leadership style, the congregation, particularly women, experience increased self-worth and empowerment through participation in church activities. Although the members do not become politically active, they find a new sense of dignity in the church and in their domestic lives. They participate in society on the personal level, strengthening the fabric of their families and communities.

The rapid growth of the Pentecostal Church is greatly impacting the neighborhood. In a *colonia* with a population of 1,500, the *Discípulos de Jesus* is in direct relationship with at least three hundred of these persons. The *rebaño* small groups and family ties would inevitably increase the number of persons that *Discípulos* is influencing on a weekly basis. The three other Pentecostal groups would further increase that influence. Father Bernardo viewed this impact as negative when he referred to Pentecostals as "ruining everything." But it is difficult to conclude from the findings of this study how Pentecostals will ultimately impact their community. However, my findings do show that the members derive meaning and found an improved quality of life since joining the Pentecostal church.

7

Observations from Ethnography

Introduction

THIS CONCLUDING CHAPTER WILL ANALYZE THE ETHNOGRAPHIC FIND-
ings and then offer some closing thoughts on the broader comparison
between the CEBs and Pentecostalism. The two previous chapters based
on my fieldwork with one local unit of the CEBs and one Pentecostal
congregation are largely descriptive. This final chapter identifies similarities and differences in the constituency, content, ecclesiology, social
action, and impact of the two movements on Mexican society. The chapter will conclude by assessing what this study has contributed to the
larger discussion of Ecclesial Base Communities and Pentecostalism in
Latin America.

My initial experience with Ecclesial Base Communities in Nicaragua and the charismatic renewal in the Methodist Church in Cuba
had sparked my interest in understanding how these two movements
could be flourishing side-by-side in Latin America. Since the CEBs
claimed to be carrying out a "preferential option for the poor," I wanted
to see what exactly was the composition of their membership and what
was the impact upon their constituencies. The Pentecostal movement
is often demeaned by mainline Protestant churches as mere fanaticism,
but it became apparent to me that there is something valuable to be
learned from their ministry among the poor. Therefore, I wanted to
study the constituency of the Pentecostal movement to see if they were
indeed working among the poor and how this group compared with the
constituency of the CEBs. Also I wanted to test the popular stereotypes
about each movement: namely, that the CEBs were a political organiza-

tion without a spiritual foundation and that Pentecostals were a vehicle for escapism without a social consciousness.

Methodology

This ethnographic field study of one local unit of a CEB and one Pentecostal church in a poor neighborhood in Cuernavaca has been helpful in eliminating many of the variables that often contaminate such comparisons across different cultures and nationalities. The socio-economic and political context of a country has considerable impact on these movements. Studying these two groups in the same poor *barrio* with the two groups located a half-block apart has helped reduce the margin of error in the study of the two constituencies. I utilized the participant-observer approach and, although I did not live in the community, I participated in mass, worship, small group meetings, pilgrimages and funerals. Nevertheless, the comparison of the ecclesiologies has not been completely parallel. The CEBs are a renewal movement within the Roman Catholic Church with no intention of separation and therefore remain responsible to the hierarchy. The Pentecostal Church, while accountable to the denominational structure of the Pentecostal Church U.S.A., is largely autonomous. Although I have carried out fieldwork simultaneously in both movements over the span of one year, it was not a longitudinal study reporting historical changes over time, rather a comparative study describing similarities and differences between the two local communities.

Composition of Membership

The strength of my methodology lies in its ability to fairly assess the constituency of each movement. All of the members of the CEB local unit were from the town of Chichioalco, Guerrero and have migrated to the *barrio*. The background of the *Discípulos* congregation is more diverse, though also largely migrant. Sixty-nine percent of the members interviewed migrated from nearby places such as Guerrero, Mexico City, and the State of Mexico, while only 31 percent are natives of Cuernavaca. While both movements, like the population of Vista Alegre as a whole, are mostly immigrants from other states, the CEBs have been in the city longer. They immigrated from Chichioalco in the 1970s and have purchased land, built their homes and raised their children here. Contrary to my early assumptions, the members of *Discípulos* were not new arrivals to Cuernavaca. The adults who had migrated to Cuernavaca averaged 20 years there—although not all those years in the neighborhood. Many had moved around seeking work and had not put down roots. Thus, the members of the Pentecostal church were somewhat more transitory and less well established than the members of the CEBs. All the members of the CEB own their own homes (albeit sometimes still under construction), while less than half (44 percent) of the adults in the Pentecostal church own their home.

With employment opportunities presumably being equal for both groups, the husbands of the CEB members were more skilled and have better established businesses than the Pentecostal men. Of course, all the CEB members were women, but their husbands and sons were mostly owners of small businesses and worked as plumbers, masons and electricians with their own tools and helpers. The Pentecostal men, in contrast, were usually helpers or employees. This naturally translated into a higher income for the men related to the CEBs. The overwhelming majority of the Pentecostal households surveyed reported an income of less than 4,000 pesos a month (U.S. $400); whereas the income of the CEBs' households ranged between 4,000 and 15,000 pesos a month (U.S. $400 to $1,500). The family income level of the married CEB women gave them the freedom to volunteer their time in the CEBs. This was not true for the women in the CEBs who were widowed, divorced or separated, whose economic situation represented the lower end of the scale. There were also Pentecostal widows who were in similarly deprived situations and benefited from the monthly food basket distributed by the church. The majority of women in both groups worked at home (housewives), although the percentage of women working outside the home was much higher in the Pentecostal church than the CEB (39 percent to 13 percent).

While almost all the CEB were women, with the exception of an occasional husband who attended out of courtesy when the meeting was in his home, the Pentecostal church was more gender balanced. This was also true for the *rebaño* small groups. As a whole, 43 percent of the adults in the congregation are men, and many of them attend with their wives and children. The Pentecostal congregation also tended to be younger, with 63 percent being less than forty years of age.

The *rebaño* groups in the Pentecostal church are similar in structure to the CEBs, although much more family-oriented. They were much more intergenerational and the average age was younger. In one *rebaño* I visited, a young man led the worship service while a young woman taught a Bible class to the children. In contrast, the average age of the CEB participants was over fifty, with no children or youth. The larger parish had many families representing a variety of age groups, but it was generally the older generation who participated in the CEBs. Occasionally the hostess of the meeting would invite her daughters and granddaughters to attend as a courtesy. The Pentecostal church, on the other hand, averaged thirty-five children in Sunday school and had a Friday night service with forty youth. The CEBs have recognized this weakness in their organization and have set ministry with youth as a national priority. While the relatively short time of my fieldwork limited my observation of how this priority might change over time, I did not personally witness any improvements in youth outreach.

Surprisingly, the Pentecostals in my study tended to have more years of schooling than the members of the CEBs. Only 50 percent of the CEB women had completed primary school and 25 percent of the women were illiterate. Of the Pentecostal adults (men and women) who participated in the survey, 42 percent had finished at least the ninth grade and only five percent were illiterate. These ratios went down slightly if only the educational level of women was considered (35 percent finishing at least ninth grade and 15 percent illiterate), but they were still higher than those of the CEB women. The educational advantage of Pentecostals could be more due to a generation than a class issue, since in recent years educational opportunities have improved across Mexican society, giving young people greater access to schools than older Mexicans. Similarly, Mexican society could have changed slightly with regard to gender, thus giving women greater opportunity to study in recent years.

In summary, my analysis of the constituencies of the two movements is that the CEBs are older, better-established, own their own homes and have a higher income (with the exception of the widowed, divorced and separated women) than the participants in the Pentecostal church. Although the members of both movements live in the same Colonia de Vista Alegre, often as neighbors, and sometime even related, the Pentecostal membership tended to be younger, newer, and more economically marginal than their CEB counterparts.

Activities of Both Groups

The CEB meetings generally were more intellectual, programmed and rational than the worship of the Pentecostal church. Although there was singing, prayer and liturgy in both movements, the primary purpose of the CEBs was to raise consciousness through Bible study reflection utilizing a clearly defined method (*to see, to judge, to act, to celebrate* and *to evaluate*). The lay *animadora* had attended a training session earlier in the week to learn the lesson for the week and had a specific goal with questions to answer. The questions required some knowledge of the Bible, politics and current events. If the *animadora* did not receive the intended answers, leading questions were asked to get the desired results. Sometimes the members felt afraid to give the wrong answer, especially in public. Nevertheless the meetings were participatory, with all having the opportunity to speak. Over time I observed the participants eventually overcoming their inhibitions and gaining confidence to speak in public.

The Pentecostal gathering was more oriented toward worship than study. The intention was to foster an environment where those present would have a spiritual/emotional encounter with the divine. Even the Wednesday evening Bible studies were set in the context of worship with a lot of singing leading up to the study. The Sunday service especially was filled with emotion, enthusiasm, and a lot of music. In spite of the pastor's command of center stage with the sermon, the whole service appeared to build up to the altar call. Not just an invitation to conversion in the classic evangelical sense, the altar call was an opportunity for all present to have an encounter with the divine. The music, motivational slogans and sermon all built up to this moment of climax. The participants, whether kneeling at the altar, praying in a corner or crying, seemed to be experiencing a moment of ecstasy, although, contrary to expectations, I did not find speaking in tongues or being "slain in the Spirit" to be common. The service was certainly enthusiastic and spontaneous, but not disorderly. There was no bulletin for the participant to follow, but the services did follow an order and a common pattern.

Leadership and Empowerment

The pastor played a central role in the leadership of the *Discípulos* congregation. While lay leaders did lead the early part of the service and played a key role in the *rebaños*, the pastor maintained an authoritarian leadership style. The congregation participated in the worship through song and occasional exclamations like *"Amen!" "Gloria a Dios!"* and *"Alleluia!"* and through their tithes and offerings. Greater participation took place in the administrative structures, such as the executive committee, *rebaños* that met in private homes, and the men's and women's organizations. The executive committee, although theoretically open to women, was entirely composed of men, although among the pastors of *rebaños* there was a fair representation of women. These leaders, such as María Morales, did give considerable time and energy to the church, leading as many as three Bible studies a week. In spite of the pastor's authoritarian leadership style, it appeared to me that the membership of the Pentecostal church was young, involved, and felt a sense of ownership and meaningful participation in the life of the church.

The CEB leadership likewise felt great ownership of their movement, although they were not as young and enthusiastic as the Pentecostal leaders. Most of the CEB leaders, from the local unit I observed, as well as others in the parish, had served as *animadores* for several years and seemed fatigued. They were quite able and committed, but found it discouraging not to see young people rise up to take their places. In the meetings, the leadership style was participatory, and the more timid women gradually gained more self-confidence to answer the questions in public. All the members of the local unit were women, as were most of the *animadores* in the parish. However the male-dominated hierarchical structure of the Roman Catholic Church reduced opportunities for leaders to emerge beyond the local unit, leading many CEB leaders to move into secular careers with non-governmental and human rights groups. The largely female make-up of the CEBs is representative of the marginal position of women within the Roman Catholic Church.[1]

---

1. One could make the case that the CEB movement has been "feminized" as a result of their powerlessness in the larger church structure. Jean and John Comaroff argue in the eighteenth century African colonial context that the "feminization" of the black other was a means of devaluation. See Comaroff and Comaroff, *Of Revelation and Revolution*, 105.

Small Groups

One of the surprises in my research was the similarity between the Pentecostal small groups and the CEBs. The methodology inherent to the CEBs and that practiced in the Pentecostal *rebaño* system are both participatory. In a small group setting one can ask questions, have dialogue and participate intimately. Due to the longevity of the CEBs' membership and to the participatory nature of their methodology, they were able to build a deeper sense of community in relation to one another. In addition to these factors, the individualism and promotion of the nuclear family in Pentecostalism were factors that inhibited a more intimate community.

Another factor contributing to trust in the CEBs could be only having women members, which was conducive to a family-style community. On one occation, Carmen's mother passed away and the meetings were cancelled for two consecutive weeks to have the rosary in her home in which all CEB members participated. In another instance the husband of a former CEB member had kidney failure and the meeting was abbreviated so that the group could visit him. These activities reflected a concern for the well-being of one another and the surrounding community.

This level of trust is just barely beginning in the Pentecostal model of *rebaños*. While newcomers were open about expressing spiritual concerns and doctrinal questions, it will take time for them to share intimate family concerns. This may also be due to the individualism inherent in Pentecostalism. The individual notion of soteriology makes persons less dependent on solidarity with the community for one's personal salvation. Nevertheless, the group dynamics of both movements contributed significantly to improve self-esteem, analytical thinking, and public speaking.

In spite of the difficulty of comparing the smaller local unit of the CEBs with the larger ecclesial structure of the Pentecostal Church, this study has shown that both movements empower their members to have greater self-esteem, dignity and sense of purpose in life. In the case of the CEBs, it is a manifest purpose of the methodology to conscienticize members to take action in society. The Pentecostal church, perhaps by latent rather than manifest intentions, produces a greater sense of dignity by virtue of one's self-understanding as a child of God and participating in a higher purpose. The small groups in both movements raise self-esteem by providing a safe space for worship, informal education and support. Individuals from the *barrio* come together to share their concerns, be affirmed and form a caring community. The group becomes a support network outside the family and outside the structure of society that has the potential to lead to transformation.

Social Action and Political Involvement

While the CEBs have a history of political involvement and solidarity with national and international causes, most of the social involvement that I observed was local. However, the local involvement I did observe—visiting the sick, notifying public health officials of a hygiene problem with stray dogs, and advocacy for regular trash pick-up by the city did improve the self-confidence of the members for potential engagement in more transcendental issues. These actions also helped to win the trust of the residents in the *barrio* for possible community action on larger issues.

Although the pastor advocated non-involvement of the church as a whole in political affairs, the overwhelming majority believed that Christians should vote in elections (although they were divided between the major parties). Although the congregation was opposed to participation in public politics, the majority noticed positive changes in their personal life, marriage and family since conversion. They also felt it was their duty as Christians to help others in need. Therefore the fabric of their lives, which interacted in the complex web of family and community, was being fortified and healed through the influence of religion in the private sphere. The Pentecostal church tended to create a potential for social action on a public level, and transforms society gradually on a private level. The self-esteem, active lay participation, and communication skills acquired through participation in the public assembly, afforded the potential for future translation into social action and political transformation in the public sphere. Although it was beyond the scope of this study, it would be telling for future research to investigate to what degree the personal transformation experienced in the Pentecostal church transfers over to social action on a public level. The empowerment and transformation of a poorer, less stable and younger sector of society has great potential for the democratization of society. It was my experience that the methodology of the CEBs was more explicit in working for social justice, yet the limited scope of their ministry with an older, gender-specific, and better-established sector of the population minimized their potential impact upon society.

Contributions of this Study

While much has been written about each of these movements and about their relationship with one another in different settings throughout Latin America, it is important to acknowledge the distinct context of each country. This study begins with a general understanding of the CEBs and Pentecostalism and then moves to the particular—in this case—one specific local unit of each movement in a poor *barrio* in Cuernavaca, Mexico. The first part of this book traces the origins of each movement generally and then focuses on their early development in Mexico. It also offers some leading theories about the growth of each phenomenon. The second part places the two movements side-by-side in an ethnographic study of a local unit of a CEB and a local congregation of a Pentecostal church. Utilizing the participant-observer methodology, the year-long field study explored how each group related to the poor. More specifically, the study identified the characteristics of persons who attended the CEBs as compared with those in the Pentecostal church. As this study has moved from the general to the specific, it does not pretend to universalize the particular, nor does it claim universal conclusions for communities located in a particular time and space.

However when I place these findings in dialogue with the body of scholarly literature some tendencies can be identified. The results of this study are consistent with other scholars (Willems, Lalive d'Epinay, and others) in the sense that the Pentecostals are working among a marginalized sector of the population. Some critics (i.e., Stoll) have questioned whether the CEBs are fulfilling their mandate of "a preferential option for the poor," while other self-critics (i.e., Mier) have acknowledged the presence of middle-class pastoral agents in the CEBs. Certainly there is not homogeneity in either the CEBs or the Pentecostals. My ethnographic findings observed a tendency for the CEB members to be working poor, but not necessarily marginalized, while the Pentecostal participants were poorer and more recent immigrants to the city.

My findings are consistent with those of Mariz with regard to participation in small groups. The involvement of the poor in small group networks, for both the CEBs and the Pentecostal church, empowers the members to cope with poverty. The opportunity to develop reading, speaking and communication skills in a small group or as part of an ecclesial structure also builds self-esteem. Since the responses to my questionnaires indicated that both the members of the CEBs and the Pentecostals perceived themselves to be better off economically now than before, these findings are consistent with Mariz's thesis that both groups are a strategic tool for coping with and perhaps overcoming poverty. This study also confirms that increased self-esteem is common to participants in both movements.

Although I would agree with Willems and Martin that Pentecostalism has the potential for social action, I would not go as far as Burdick to affirm that the Pentecostal churches are already more effective than the CEBs in creating positive social change. This may have been his experience in northeastern Brazil, but is not consistent with my findings in Mexico. The Pentecostals are, however, creating social changes in the private sphere as the majority of the members perceive an improved quality of life in their family, marriage and economic situation. This is consistent with the view of Mariz and Peterson regarding the microsocial impact of Pentecostalism upon society.

Although the Pentecostal worship service is more emotional and less intellectual than the CEB meeting, contrary to stereotypes it does have order and reason. In the spirit of Weber, Martin and Mariz, I would concur that the rationalization of religion does contribute to the democratization, modernization and development of society. To the degree that rationalization is present in both movements, they contribute to self-discipline, individual initiative, and participatory decision-making. Certainly the CEBs use analysis and reason in their methodology. Likewise the members Pentecostal church, in spite of the emotional worship setting, acquire analytical and communication skills, and thus become equipped to participate in the democratization of society. What makes the potential social change of Pentecostalism so significant for Latin American is the magnitude of the movement— particularly among the poor. The change may already be occurring on the micro or private level of personal and family relationships, but it is yet to be seen whether this potential for concrete social change and democratization will be realized on a larger scale in society.

Finally, there is still much to be learned about the impact on society of each of these significant ecclesial movements. This study has shown that neither the CEBs nor Pentecostalism are easily predictable, nor do they fit the preconceived stereotypes. They are neither contradictory, nor are they different flavors of the same essence. Those interested in Latin America, social justice and the interplay between religion and politics cannot ignore the impact of these movements. They will continue to be present in Latin American society impacting the religious and political fabric of the region. As a researcher I have come to respect the participants in both movements who give time and energy to advance their respective causes, and thereby contribute, intentionally or unintentionally, to a more democratic society. I further admire them for their commitment to work among the poor in Latin America when many mainline Protestant denominations have opted for the more comfortable path of ministry within the middle-class.

Bibliography

Adriance, Madeleine. "Organic Intellectuals and Basic Communities." Department of Sociology, University of Massachusetts, paper presented at the Annual Meeting of the Society for the Scientific Study of Religion, Chicago, IL, October 26–28, 1984.

Alvarez, Carmelo E., editor. *Pentecostalismo y Liberación: Una Experiencia Latino-americana*, San Jose: DEI, 1992.

————. *The Protestant Movement in Central America*. New York: Friendship, 1990.

————. *El Protestantismo Latinoamericano: Entre la Crisis y el Desafío*. San Jose: DEI, 1993.

————. *Santidad y Compromiso*. México, D.F.: CUPSA, 1985.

Anderson, Benedict. *Imagined Communities*. New York: Verso, 1983.

Aragón, Rafael, and Eberhard Loschcke. *La Iglesia de Los Pobres en Nicaragua: Historia y Perspectivas*. Managua, Nicaragua: Rafael Aragón y Eberhard Loschcke, 1991.

Arce, Reinerio, and Manuel Quintero. *Carismatismo en Cuba*. Quito: CIAI, 1997.

Azevedo, Marcello. *Basic Ecclesial Communities in Brazil: The Challenge of a New Way of Being Church*. Washington, DC: Georgetown University Press, 1987.

Balibar, Etienne, and Immanuel Wallerstein. *Race, Nation, Class: Ambiguous Identities*. New York: Verso, 1991.

Barreiro, Alvaro. *Basic Ecclesial Communities: The Evangelization of the Poor*. Maryknoll, NY: Orbis, 1982.

Bastian, Jean-Pierre. *Protestantismos y Modernidad Latinoamericana: Historia de Unas Minorías Religiosas Activas en América Latina*. México, D.F.: Fondo de Cultura Económica, 1994.

Bavarel, Michel. *New Communities, New Ministries: The Church Resurgent in Africa, Asia, and Latin America*. Maryknoll, NY: Orbis, 1980.

Berger, Peter L. *Pyramids of Sacrifice: Political Ethics and Social Change*. Garden City, NY: Anchor, 1974.

Berger, Peter L., and Thomas Luckman. *The Social Construction of Reality*. Garden City, NY: Doubleday, 1966.

Berryman, Philip. "Latin America: Iglesia que Nace del Pueblo." *Christianity and Crisis* 41:14 (1981).

Beto, Frey, and Carlos Alberto Libanio C. *Lo que son Las Comunidades Eclesiales de Base*. Bogota, Colombia: Indo American Press Service, 1981.

Beto, Frey, Pablo Richard, and Leonardo Boff. *Fe y Política*. n.d.

Boff, Clodovis, and Leonardo Boff. *Introducing Liberation Theology*. Maryknoll, NY: Orbis, 1998 (1986).

Boff, Leonardo. *Church: Charism and Power: Liberation Theology and the Institutional Church*. New York: Crossroad, 1990.

————. *Ecclesiogenesis: The Base Communities Reinvent the Church*. Maryknoll, NY: Orbis, 1986.

————. *Jesus Christ Liberator: A Critical Christology for Our Time*. Maryknoll, NY: Orbis, 1979.

————. *Passion of Christ, Passion of the World*. Maryknoll, NY: Orbis, 1987.

————. *Trinity and Society*. Maryknoll, NY: Orbis, 1997.

Bonilla, Antonio. "Breve Historia del Congreso y Asembleas, 1932–1972." México: Iglesia de Dios, Evangelio Completo en México (November, 1972).

Boudewijnse, Barbara, Andre Droogers, and Frans Kamsteeg. *Algo Más Que Opio: Una Lectura Antropológica del Pentecostalismo Latinoamericano y Caribeño*. San José: DEI, 1991.

Bowen, Kurt. *Evangelism and Apostasy: The Evolution and Impact of Evangelicals in Modern Mexic*. Montreal: McGill-Queen's University Press, 1996.

Brown, Robert McAfee. *Unexpected News: Reading the Bible with Third World Eyes*. Phila-delphia: Westminster, 1984.

Bruno, Daniel A. "Ecclesiola in Ecclesia: Crítica y Renovación de la Iglesia. El Pietismo del Siglo XVII y las Comunidades de Base." *Cuadernos de Teología* 20 (2001) 315–42.

Burdick, John. *Looking for God in Brazil: The Progressive Catholic Church in Urban Brazil's Religious Arena*. Berkeley: University of California Press, 1993.

Burgess, Stanley M., and Gary B. McGee, editors. *Dictionary of Pentecostal and Charismatic Movements*. Grand Rapids: Zondervan, 1988.

Busco, Elizabeth E. *The Reformation of Machismo: Evangelical Conversion and Gender in Colombia*. Austin: University of Texas Press, 1995.

Cabestrero Teofilo. *Blood of The Innocent: Victims of the Contras' War in Nicaragua*. Maryknoll, NY: Orbis, 1985.

Caminemos Juntos. Misión por la Fraternidad 2001, Tiempo de Adviento y Navidad, n.d.

Campos, Bernardo. *De la Reforma Protestante a la Pentecostalidad de La Iglesia: Debate sobre el Pentecostalismo en América Latina*. Quito, Equador: Ediciones CLAI, 1997.

Cardinal, Ernesto. *The Gospel of Solentiname*. 4 vols. Maryknoll, NY: Orbis, 1976, 1978, 1979, 1982.

————. *Religiao e Clases Populares*. Rio de Janeiro: Editora Vozes, 1980.

Cleary, Edward, and Hannah Stewart-Gambino. *Power Politics and Pentecostals in Latin America*. Boulder, CO: Westview, 1998.

Clifford, James. *The Predicament of Culture*. Cambridge: Harvard University Press, 1988.

Comaroff, Jean and John. *Of Revelation and Revolution*. Vol. 1: *Christianity, Colonialism and Consciousness in South Africa*. Chicago: University of Chicago Press, 1991.

Committee of Santa Fe. "A New Inter-American Policy for the Eighties." Washington, DC: Council for the Inter-American Security, 1980.

————. "Santa Fe II: A Strategy for Latin America in the Nineties." Washington, DC: Council for the Inter-American Security, 1988.

Comunidades Eclesiales de Base. *Cantemos en Comunidad*. Cuernavaca: Diocesis de Cuernavaca, 1982.

———. "A, B, C de la Biblia." Managua, Nicaragua, n.d.

Concha Malo, Miguel, Oscar González Gari, and Lino F. Salas. *La Participación de los Cristianos en el Proceso Popular de Liberación en México (1968–1983)*. México, D.F.: Siglo Veintiuno Editores, 1986.

Cook, William, Jr. "The Expectation of the Poor: A Protestant Missiological Study of the Catholic 'Comunidades de Base' in Brazil." PhD diss., Fuller Theological Seminary, 1982.

———. *The Expectation of the Poor: Latin America Base Ecclesial Communities in a Protestant Perspective*. Maryknoll, NY: Orbis, 1985.

———, editor. *New Face of the Church in Latin America*. Maryknoll, NY: Orbis, 1994.

Cox, Harvey. *Fire from Heaven: the Rise of Pentecostal Spirituality and the Reshaping of Religion in the Twenty-First Century*. Reading, MA: Addison-Wesley, 1995.

Cristianos Nicaragüenses por los Pobres. XIII Assembly, February 5–7, 1999.

Cruz, Guadalupe. *Mujeres de CEBs Identidad y Promesa*. México, D.F.: Centro de Estudios Ecuménicos, n.d.

Dayton, Donald W. *Theological Roots of Pentecostalism*. Grand Rapids: Francis Asbury, 1987.

De Santa Ana, Julio. *Protestantismo, Cultura y Sociedad: Problemas y Perspectivas de la Fe Evangélica en América Latina*. Buenos Aires: Editorial La Aurora, 1970.

"Defender Nuestro Derecho a la Rebelión." *Barricada Internacional* 339 (July, 1991) 1.

Deiros, Pablo A., and Carlos Mraida. *Latinoamérica en Llamas*. Miami: Editorial Caribe, 1994.

D'Epinay, Christian Lalive. *Haven of the Masses: A Study of the Pentecostal Movement in Chile*. London: Luttherworth, 1969.

———. *Religión e Ideología en una Perspectiva Sociológico*. Río Piedras, Puerto Rico: S.E.P.R. 1973.

Diamond, Sara. *Spiritual Warfare: The Politics of the Christian Right*. Boston: South End, 1990.

Dioceses of Cuernavaca. *Don Sergio, 25 Años de Obispo*. Guía del Año Jubilar, Cuernavaca: Dioceses of Cuernavaca, 1976.

Documentos Completos de Vaticano II. Santander, Spain: Sal Terrae, 1967.

"Dogmatic Constitution of the Church." *Documents of the Second Vatican Council*. Rome: 1965.

Duque, José, editor. *La Tradición Protestante en la Teología Latinoamericana: Lectura de La Tradición Metodista*. San José: DEI, 1983.

Ecumenical Center Antonio Valdivieso. "Nicaraguan Revolutionary Christians Face The Crisis of Civilization." Managua, Nicaragua, 1988.

Emge, Donald Raymond. "Critical Thinking within a Religious Context: An Analysis of the History and Methodology of the Liberatory Comunidades Eclesiales de Base, Cuernavaca, Mexico, 1967–1990." PhD diss., Kansas State University, 1990.

Equipo de Educación Maíz. "Comunidades Cristianas." El Salvador, 1989.

Escobar, Samuel, Estuardo McIntosh, and Juan Inocencia, editors. *Historia y Misión: Revisión de Perspectivas*. Lima, Peru: Ediciones Presencia, 1994.

Equipo Nacional, Comunidades Eclesiales de Base. "Retos Nacionales 2000–2004." Tenayuca, No.350, Col. Santa Cruz Atoyac, México, D.F. 03310, n.d.

Espin, Orlando O. "Pentecostalism and Popular Catholicism: The Poor and *Traditio*." *Journal of Hispanic/Latino Theology* 3:2 (1995) 14–43.

Fernandes, Luisa. "Basic Christian Communities in the Brazilian Context." Harvard University, Graduate School of Education, paper presented at the Society of Scientific Studies on Religion, October 26–28, 1984.

Fernandes, Rubem Cesar. "O Debate entre Sociólogos a Propósito dos Pentecostais." *Cadernos do I.S.E.R.* 6 (1984) 49–60.

Foucault, Michel. *Power/Knowledge: Selected Interviews and Other Writings, 1972–1977.* Edited and translated by Colin Gorden. New York: Pantheon, 1980.

Floristan, Casiano. *Vaticano II: Un Concilio Pastoral.* Salamanca: Ediciones Sígueme, 1990.

Freire, Paulo. *Pedagogy of the Oppressed.* New York: Continuum, 1986.

Galeano, Eduardo. *Open Veins of Latin America,* Mexico, D.F.: Siglo XXI Editores, 1997.

Gaxiola, Manuel J. *La Serpiente y La Paloma: Análisis del Crecimiento de La Iglesia Apostólica de la Fe en Cristo Jesús de México.* South Pasadera: William Carey Library, 1970.

Geertz, Clifford. *The Interpretation of Culture.* New York: Basic, 1973.

Gerlach, L. P. "Pentecostalism: Revolution or Counterrevolution?" In *Religious Movements in Contemporary America,* edited by I. Zaretsky and M.P. Leone. Princeton, NJ: Princeton University Press, 1974.

Gerlach, L. P., and Virginia Hine. *Lifeway Leaps: The Dynamics of Change in America.* Minneapolis: University of Minnesota Press, 1973.

———. *People, Power and Change: Movements of Social Transformation.* Indianapolis: Bob Merrill, 1970.

Girardi, Giulio, and Leticia Renteria Chavez, editors. *Don Sergio Méndez Arceo: Patriarca de la Solidaridad Liberadora.* México, D.F.: Ediciones DABAR, 2000.

Gonzalez, Justo. *Mañana: Christian Theology from a Hispanic Perspective.* Nashville: Abingdon, 1990.

Guerrero, Andres G. *A Chicano Theology.* Maryknoll, NY: Orbis, 1987.

Gutiérrez, Benjamin F. *En La Fuerza del Espíritu: Los Pentecostales en América Latina: Un Desafío a las Iglesias Históricas.* México, D.F.: AIPRAL, 1995.

Gutierrez, Gustavo. *A Theology of Liberation.* Maryknoll, NY: Orbis, 1971.

"Historia de La Iglesia de los Pobres en Nicaragua." Managua, Nicaragua: El Tayacan, n.d.

"Historia de la Parroquia San Pablo Apóstol." Managua, Nicaragua: Parroquia San Pablo Apostil, n.d.

Hoffman, Virginia. "Leonardo Boff, *Ecclesiogenesis: The Base Communities Reinvent the Church.*" Unpublished paper presented for a Colloquium at Garrett-Evangelical Theological Seminary, December 13, 1991.

Hollenweger, Walter. "After 20 Years Research on Pentecostalism." *International Review of Mission* 75 (1986) 297.

———. *The Pentecostals.* Peabody, MA: Hendrickson, 1988.

Hopkins, Dwight N. *Black Theology of Liberation.* Maryknoll, NY: Orbis, 1999.

Isasi-Diaz, Ada Maria. *Hispanic Women: Prophetic Voice in the Church.* Mineapolis: Fortress, 1992.

————. *Mujerista Theology.* Maryknoll, NY: Orbis, 1997.

Jennings, Theodore W. *Good News to the Poor: John Wesley's Evangelical Economics.* Nashville: Abingdon, 1990.

————."Good News to the Poor in the Wesleyan Heritage." In *Theology and Evangelism in the Wesleyan Heritage,* edited by James Logan. Nashville: Kingswood, 1994.

Jiménez López, Bertoldo. "Historia de la Iglesia de Dios en México." Evangelio Completo. A.R. México, n.d.

Johns, Cheryl B. *Pentecostal Formation: A Pedagogy among the Oppressed.* Sheffield, UK: Sheffield Academic, 1993.

Kairos, Central America. *A Challenge To The Churches of The World.* New York: Theology in Global Context Program, 1988.

Kickham, Larry. "Holy Spirit or Holy spook?" *Covert Action Information Bulletin* 27 (1987) 4.

Kirkpatrick, Dow. *The Holy Spirit.* Nashville: Tidings, 1974.

Lancaster, Roger. *Thanks to God and the Revolution: Popular Religion and Class Consciousness in the New Nicaragua.* New York: Columbia University Press, 1988.

LeFevre, Perry, editor. "Base Christian Communities." *The Chicago Theological Seminary Register: A Professional Journal for Ministers* 81 (1991) 1–9.

Lewis, Oscar. *The Children of Sanchez: Autobiography of a Mexican Family.* New York: Vintage, 1961.

Libanio, J. B., and Alfonso Murad. *Introducción a la Teología: Perfiles, Enfoques, Tareas,* México, D.F.: DABAR, 1996.

Maccise, Camilo. *La Teología de La Liberación.* Bogota, Colombia: Paulinas, 1989.

MacEoin, Gary. "Puebla: Moment of Decision for the Latin American Church." *Cross Currents* 28 (1978).

MacEoin, Gary, and Nivita Riley. *Puebla: A Church Being Born.* New York: Paulist, 1980.

Maciel, Roberto. *Caminemos Juntos: Por el tiempo de adviento y navidad.* México: Misión por la Fraternidad, Christmas, 2000–2001.

Mackay, Juan A. *El Otro Cristo Español.* México, D.F.: CUPSA, 1993.

Maduro, Otto. *Religión y Lucha de Clases.* Caracas, Venezuala: Editorial Ateneo de Caracas, 1979.

Marins, José. *Basic Ecclesial Community: Church from the Roots.* Quito, Equador: Colegio Técnico Don Bosco, n.d.

Mariz, Cecilia. *Coping with Poverty: Pentecostals and Christian Base Communities in Brazil.* Philadelphia: Temple University Press, 1994.

Márquez, Martin, and Anton Martínez Riquelme. *Comunidades Cristianas de Jovenes: Experiencia y Proyecto de Trabajo de Cinco Parroquias de Murcia.* Madrid: PPC, 1982.

Martin, David. *Pentecostalism: The World Their Parish.* Oxford: Blackwell, 2002.

————. *Tongues of Fire: The Explosion of Protestantism in Latin America.* Cambridge, MA: Blackwell, 1990.

Martínez, Abelino. *Las Sectas en Nicaragua: Oferta y Demanda de Salvación.* San José: D.E.I. 1989.

Marx, Karl. *El Capital: Crítica de la Economía Política.* Translated by Wenceslao Roces. México, D.F.: Fundo de Cultura Económica, 1946.

McClung, Grant. *Azusa Street and Beyond: Pentecostal Missions and Church Growth in the 20th Century.* New Jersey: Bridge, 1986.

McEllhenney, John G., editor. *United Methodism in America: A Compact History,* Nashville: Abingdon, 1992.

McGavran, Donald. *El Crecimiento de la Iglesia en México.* México, D.F.: CUPSA, 1966.

Melendez, Guillermo. *Seeds of Promise: The Prophetic Church in Central America.* New York: Friendship, 1990.

Méndez Arceo, Don Sergio. "Recuperando la Memoria de Don Sergio Méndez Arceo." Cuernavaca: Fundación Don Sergio Méndez Arceo, 2000.

Merton, Robert K. *Social Theory and Social Structure.* Glencoe, IL: Free, 1957.

Microsoft Encarta Dictionary. New York: Bedford St. Martin's, 2002.

Miguez Bonino, José. *Rostros del Protestantismo Latinoamericano.* Buenos Aires: Nueva Creación, 1995.

Miller, Donald. *Coming of Age: Protestantism in Latin America.* Landham, MA: University Press of America, 1994.

Miller, Frank C. *Old Villages and a New Town: Industrialization in Mexico.* Reading, MA: Cummings, 1973.

Mier, Sebastián. *Las Comunidades Eclesiales de Base: Los Pobres como Sujeto de su Historia.* México, D.F.: DABAR, 2001.

Miranda, Jose. *Marx and the Bible: A Critique of the Philosophy of Oppression.* Maryknoll, NY: Orbis, 1974.

Moltmann, Jürgen. *The Open Church: Invitation to a Messianic Lifestyle.* SCM, 1978.

———. *The Passion for Life.* Philadelphia: Fortress, 1978.

Montero, Maritz. *Psicología Política Latinoamericana.* Caracas: Editorial PANAPO, 1987.

Montgomery, Thomas. *Rice and Beans and Hope.* New York: Circus, 1988.

Mulligan, Joseph. *The Nicaraguan Church and the Revolution.* Kansas City: Sheed & Ward, 1991.

Musser, Donald W., and Joseph L. Price, editors. *A New Handbook of Christian Theology.* Nashville: Abingdon, 1992.

Myers, William R. *Research in Ministry.* Chicago: Exploration, 1993.

National Federation of Priests' Councils. *Basic Christian Communities: The United States Experience.* Vatican City: Costello, 1965.

———. *Developing Basic Christian Communities.* Vatican City: Costello, 1965.

Nida, Eugene A. "The Indigenous Churches in Latin America." *Practical Anthropology* 8:3 (1961) 97–105.

Niebuhr, H. Richard. *The Social Sources of Denominationalism.* New York: Holt & Rinehart, 1929.

Nuij, Tom. "Introducción a la Lectura de la Biblia." Curso de la Escuela de Formación, CEB, n.d.

Otero, Luis Leñero, María Estela Fernández, and María Teresa Guzmán. "Investigación de Autodiagnóstico sobre el Fortalecimiento de las CEB." Instituto Mexicano de Estudios Sociales, A.C. Enero, 2001.

"Pastoral Evangelizadora: Evangelización en Pueblos Nuevos." CEPAS, Curso de Educación Pastoral. San José, Costa Rica, 1991.

"Pastoral de la Espiritualidad: Hacia una Liturgia Latinoamericana que Afirme la Vida." CEPAS, Curso de Educación Pastoral, San José, Costa Rica, 1991.

Parroquia La Cruz. "Como Poner Nuestros Talentos al Servicio de la Comunidad?" Managua: Oficina de Justicia y Paz, August 1991.

――――. "Tenemos los Ingredientes para Preparar las CEBs, pero nos Faltan los Instrumentos." Managua: Oficina de Justicia y Paz, March 1992.

――――. "Trabajamos Hombro a Hombro con la Mirada Puesta en Dios." Managua: Oficina de Justicia y Paz, March 1990–May 1991.

Paul, Garrett E. "Basic Christian Communities." In *A New Handbook of Christian Theology,* edited by Donald W. Musser and Joseph Price. Nashville: Abingdon, 1992.

Peterson, Douglas. *Not by Might, Nor by Power: A Pentecostal Theology of Social Concern in Latin America.* Oxford: Regnum, 1996.

Pérez, Marcelino, S.J. *Valores Humanos y Métodos de Trabajo del Dirigente Popular.* Panama: CEASPA, 1986.

Pierce-Bomann, Rebecca. *Faith in the Barrios: The Pentecostal Poor in Bogota.* Lynne Rienner, 2000.

"Que es Encuentros Cristianos?" Guatemala: Encuentros Cristianos, n.d.

"¿Que son? Las Comunidades Eclesiales de Base." México, D.F.: Ediciones DABAR, 1992.

Rebasa, Emilio O., and Gloria Caballero. *Mexicano: Esta es tu constitución.* México: Miguel Ángel Porrua Grupo Editorial, 1997.

Rentaría Chávez, Leticia, and Giulio Girardi. *Don Sergio Méndez Arceo: Patriarca de la Solidaridad Liberadora.* México, D.F.: Ediciones DABAR, 2000.

Richard, Pablo. *La Fuerza Espiritual de La Iglesia de Los Pobres.* San José, Costa Rica: Departamento Ecuménico de Investigaciones, 1987.

Rolim, Francisco Cartaxo. *O Que E O Pentecostalismo.* Brasilia: Editora Basiliense, 1987.

――――. *Religião e Classes Populares.* Petrópolis: Vozes, 1980.

Rosaldo, Renato. *Culture and Truth: the Remaking of Social Analysis.* Boston: Beacon, 1989.

Rosales, Alberto. *Estado e Iglesia en México: Legislación Religiosa.* México, D.F.: Ravena, 1990.

Ruether, Rosemary Radford. "Basic Communities: Renewal at the Roots." *Christianity and Crisis* 41:14 (1981) 232–37.

――――. *Liberation Theology: Human Hope Confronts Christian History and American Power.* New York: Paulist, 1972.

Runyon, Theodore. *Revivalism and Social Reform.* Nashville: Abingdon, 1957.

――――. *Sanctification and Liberalism.* Nashville: Abingdon, 1981.

Said, Edward W. *Culture and Imperialism.* New York: Vintage, 1994.

――――. *Orientalism.* New York: Vintage, 1978.

Saravia, Javier. *Comunidades en Camino.* México, D.F.: Centro de Reflexión Teológica, n.d.

――――. *La Biblia.* México, D.F.: Centro de Reflexión Teológica, 1979.

Schafer, Heinrick. *Protestantismo y Crisis Social en América Central.* San José: DEI, 1992.

Secretariado Internacional de Solidaridad. "Oscar Romero." *Iglesia y Liberación de los Pueblos.* México D.F.: Ediciones Nuevomar, 1984.

Segundo, Juan Lui. *Liberación de la Teología.* Buenos Aires, Argentina: Carlos Lohse, 1975.

Shaull, Richard, and Waldo Cesar. *Pentecostalism and the Future of the Christian Churches.* Grand Rapids: Eerdmans, 2000.

Sobrino, Jon. *Cristología desde América Latina.* San Salvador: ECE, 1977.

Sobrino, Jon, and Juan Hernández Pico. *Teología de la Solidaridad Cristiana,* Managua: Centro Ecuménico Antonio Valdivieso, 1983.

Spener, Philip Jacob. *Pia Desideria.* Philadelphia: Fortress, 1964.

Stam, John. *The Use of the Bible in Central American Base Communities, When you Pass through the Waters.* Managua, Nicaragua: CEBS, n.d.

Stoll, David. *Is Latin America Turning Protestant? The Politics of Evangelical Growth.* Berkeley: University of California Press, 1990.

Suenen, Cardinal L. Joseph, and D. Helder Camara. *Charismatic Renewal and Social Action: A Dialogue.* Ann Arbor, MD: Servant, 1972.

Suurmond, Jean-Jaques. *Word and Spirit at Play: Towards a Charismatic Theology.* Grand Rapids: Eerdmans, 1994.

Swedish, Margaret. "Encountering the Poor-Challenge of Faith." *Basta* (July 1990) 44.

Synan, V. *Aspects of Pentecostal Charismatic Origins.* Plainfield, NJ: Logos, 1975.

———. *The Holiness-Pentecostal Movement.* Grand Rapids: Eerdmans, 1971.

———. *In the Latter Days.* Ann Arbor: Servant, 1984.

Tamez Elsa. "Quetzalcoatl y El Dios Cristiano: Amianza y Lucha de Dioses." *Literary Backgrounds,* n.d.

Tanner, Kathryn. *Theories of Culture: A New Agenda for Theology.* Minneapolis: Fortress, 1997.

Taussig, Michael T. *The Devil and Commodity Fetishism in South America.* Chapel Hill: University of North Carolina Press, 1980.

Teilhard de Chardin, Pierre. *The Phenomenon of Man.* New York: Harper, 1959.

Thijssen, Gerardo, and Solia Luna, editors. *Recuperando la Memoria de Don Sergio Mendez Arceo.* México: Fundación Don Sergio Méndez Arceo, 2000.

Tillich, Paul. *Love, Power and Justice.* Oxford: Oxford University Press, 1954.

Vorres, Sergio, and John Eagleson. *The Challenge of Basic Christian Communities.* Maryknoll, NY: Orbis, 1982.

Vigil, José Maria, and Ángel Torrellas. *Misas Centroamericanas: Transcripción y Comentario Teológico.* CAV-CEBES, 1988.

Villafane, Eldin. *The Liberating Spirit: Toward an Hispanic American Pentecostal Social Ethic.* Grand Rapids: Eerdmans, 1993.

UCA Editores. *Medellín: Los Textos de Medellín y el Proceso de Cambio en América Latina.* San Salvador, El Salvador: UCA, 1985.

Weber, Max. *The Protestant Ethic and the Spirit of Capitalism.* New York: Routledge, 1992.

———. *The Sociology of Religion.* Boston: Beacon, 1963.

Willems, Emilio. *Followers of the New Faith: Cultural Change and the Rise of Protestantism in Brazil and Chile.* Nashville: Vanderbilt University Press, 1967.

Wingeier-Rayo, Philip. "The 18th Century Early Methodist Revival and the Renewal of the Methodist Church in Cuba: A Comparative Study." MA thesis, Garrett-Evangelical Theological Seminary, 1997.

Wingeier-Rayo, Philip, and Paul Chilcote. "The Wesleyan Revival and Methodism in Cuba." *Quarterly Review* 17 (1997) 207–22.

Zenteno, Arnaldo. *Ejercicios Desde Los Pobres.* Managua: CEBs, 1991.

Index

Altar call, 126, 127, 131, 138, 144
Anomie, 5, 20, 21, 24–26, 33, 75
Azusa Street, 5, 10, 13, 14

Bastian, Jean-Pierre, 5, 19, 21, 24,
    25, 28, 33, 68, 69, 70, 77
Bible (Bible Studies), 1, 2, 17, 40 44,
    45, 51, 57, 66, 72, 92, 93, 103,
    114, 122, 131, 135, 136, 138,
    144, 156, 158
Boff, Leonardo, 5, 40, 43–47, 49, 56,
    71, 78, 94
Brazil, viii, 5, 15, 21, 25–27, 30, 36,
    38–40, 42–44, 48, 49, 57–61,
    64–68, 73, 75, 77, 93, 149
Brusco, Elizabeth, 31, 78

CELAM (Council of Latin
    American Bishops,
    Medellin), 3, 35, 41–44, 51,
    57, 63, 95, 158
Charismatic renewal, 3, 94, 140
Chile, 50, 57, 58, 75
Civic/Social/public engagement,
    24, 77, 135, 147
Communism (Communist), 1, 29,
    36, 37, 76
Conscientization (Conscienticize),
    66, 72, 76, 77, 79, 146
Cuba, 2, 3, 37, 38, 50, 140

Democracy (pluralism, pluraliza-
    tion), 4, 5, 21, 23, 33, 37, 70,
    74

Education (school, schooling), 2,
    12, 13, 16, 21, 24, 27, 37, 62,
    72, 88, 94, 96, 107, 120, 122,
    123, 125, 127, 128, 134, 137,
    138, 143, 147
Eschatology, x, 28
Ethnography (ethnographic), 5, 6,
    27, 58, 80, 82, 83, 84, 86–88,
    91, 114, 117, 140, 141, 148

Freire, Paulo, 49, 73
Fundamentalism, 14

Gift of the Spirit (gifts), 13, 19, 27,
    40, 66, 67
Glossolalia (speaking in tongues),
    12, 13, 18, 19, 26, 66, 67, 69,
    127, 144

Hermeneutical circle, 54, 73
Holiness movement, 1, 10, 11, 14,
    74
Hollenweger, Walter, 12, 13, 15, 16
Holy Spirit, x, 11, 12, 14–19, 22, 26,
    27, 66, 67, 72, 129, 130, 131,
    135

Johns, Cheryl Bridges, 10, 11, 74, 79

Lay (laity, Delegates of the Word),
    x, ix, 22, 27, 35, 38–42, 48, 49,
    52, 57, 63, 71–73, 85, 91, 93,
    95, 101, 102, 118, 120,